VENERABLE WOMEN

Honor, love, respect,
Dawn Morningstar

VENERABLE WOMEN

Transform Ourselves
Transform the World

DAWN MORNINGSTAR

ISBN: 978-0-9982111-3-8

Cover design: Elder Carson
Author photo: Ashley Rick
Editor: Marly Cornell

Venerable Women LLC
venerablewomen.com

For Rosie, Joan, Lauren, and Lindsay, and my mother, Vicky, who unwittingly inspired this movement.

Venerable Women is an offering of the heart.

"The morning arrives
and the song of a bird comes undone.
I imagine for the first time in my life
that its wings
are my own."
—*Corrine De Winter*

CONTENTS

INTRODUCTION

I stood in the middle of my kitchen with arms outstretched to the heavens, tears rolling down my cheeks. Calling out to all the women who ever lived and all the women yet to be born, I asked, "How can I serve women so that each of us may live our highest and best lives? What wisdom can you share with me? I am your willing scribe. I want to be your voice."

I knew an answer would come, and it did as my gel pen glided across the paper. What I wrote that day on the pages in front of me took my breath away. And now, continuing ripples emanate in response to my plea.

⚜ ⚜ ⚜

Ever since I heard what the Dalai Lama said at the Vancouver Peace Summit in 2009, "The world will be saved by the Western woman," his words ignited a new sense of hope in me. My heart was immediately enlisted in making those words come true.

I am blessed in so many ways as a Western woman in the twenty-first century. I have plentiful food and water, clothing and shelter, a peaceful environment, and possibilities. Though I am more grateful for those gifts than I can say, I know that having the basic needs of life is not the reality for so many of my brothers and sisters around the globe.

Reflect on the word *saved* in Dalai Lama's comment: "The world will be *saved* by the Western woman." To *save* means to keep safe, deliver, emancipate, and liberate. Surely each of us longs for freedom.

My own painful beginning in this life set me on a search to be saved. Abandonment, betrayal, confusion, and abuse describe my first years of life. As I grew up, I became enmeshed in codependent relationships that could have been examples in Melody Beattie's book *Codependent No More.* One of many things I learned from that book was that my naïve attempt to save others and focus on their needs, without first trying to save myself, derailed me from being my most evolved and best self. Learning that lesson changed the course of my life and the lives of many others along my path.

What happens when a woman does not pay attention to her own needs while she gives, and gives, and gives to others? Have you ever seen that happen to someone you know? Have you been that woman yourself at some point in your life?

Women are realizing that the quality of our giving—to our loved ones, our causes, our work, our world, and a multitude of other commitments—is only as good as what we decide to give to ourselves. We are noticing that what happens to *each* of us, directly and profoundly, affects *all* of us. That is one of the profound secrets to saving the world, our "secret sauce" so to speak: we must start *within* ourselves, seeing that our own needs are fulfilled first, before directing our attention to the needs and wants of others. Doing so elevates the quality of all we are, all we experience, all we do and, just as importantly, all we give.

When we give from a place of being fulfilled ourselves, we avoid the very real outcome that occurs if we give from a place of lack and end up resenting those we desired to help in the first place. Rather than giving from depleted energy and resources, authentic giving from that juicy, creative, full part of ourselves makes us feel jubilant about our giving.

In surveys, research, and observations made while interviewing leaders, activists, and educators on my radio talk show in the 2000s, I discovered this common thread: all humans benefit wildly when we feel heard, valued, loved, and needed. We all yearn to feel significant. We thrive when we have deep connections with others. When our needs are fully met, we naturally have more to give. Our efforts to serve and to make a difference become filled with grace and ease.

Ahh. Doesn't *that* feel good?

⚜ ⚜ ⚜

Saving the world is surely a noble and huge undertaking. However, for the Western woman to accept such a mission is not only possible, it's necessary and timely. Brothers and sisters around the globe share the responsibility of transforming our world and do so every day. But Western women are uniquely positioned to respond to the Dalai Lama's prophecy. Most of us have what we require from a basic needs perspective—and then some. In fact, a lot of women feel a growing need for a simpler life and to own less *stuff*. Many have longed for something they could not name—something much higher up on Maslow's hierarchy of needs.

We know we want to help, we want to make a difference, and we want to feel better in our own lives, too. We are awakening, opening our eyes and hearts. We sense an inner knowing. A Golden Age is upon us that cannot be based on old paradigms or beliefs that no longer work, if they ever did.

An astrological "shift," as some call it, moved our planet after thousands of years from the Age of Pisces, ruled by the masculine principle, to the Age of Aquarius that is ruled by the feminine. The actual transition date was December 21, 2012, the last day on the Mayan calendar. The world became positioned to embody the feminine principles of love, compassion, and spirit.

Most current world religions originated in the Iron Age and were based in mental concepts about a God "out there somewhere," certainly not inside of each of us. In this new paradigm, having only just stepped into the potential of this Golden Age, we still see a strong pull to defend what people once felt safe believing.

Many people are waking up to the calling of their souls to serve, enlighten, and be confident in spiritual and consciousness awakening. Women's ears are closer to the ground, closer to Mother Earth. Women's oneness with the Divine is being made manifest on earth. Now is the time for women to stand in the fullness of our best selves and create a world in which all of life matters and is valued in rich and loving ways.

With more than twenty years coaching women individually and in groups, within large and small circles and before audiences, I am continually reminded that women need to first save *our own* world in order to save *the* world. For years I've heard a few common underlying messages that woman after woman conveyed in one form or another.

- I'm not always sure what I want or need or if it's even possible to have my needs met.
- I do not feel worthy of having what I desire.
- I feel alone on my journey.
- I become frustrated after working toward personal transformation and finding myself right back where I started.

We must say farewell to lonely journeys—and hello to loving connection and joy with others who desire a kind and loving world. We must liberate and deliver ourselves. We begin by acknowledging and filling our own needs. This process inevitably brings joy and fulfillment to a point of overflowing, which naturally impacts the world in wholesome, nourishing ways.

We pray for and bless others, volunteer our services when and where we can, and support causes we believe in. As we do these things, we make sure our resources of all kinds—money, energy, time, and attention—are inner- and outer-focused in a balanced measure.

For women to be keepers of the seeds of loving-kindness leading this worthy cause is not to over-take anyone else. Instead, by circulating those seeds across the landscape of human consciousness and collaborating with others, we create greater harmony in the agreements we make and in the world we actualize.

Imagine our world populated by multitudes of jubilant, whole, venerable women and men. By *vénérable* I mean worthy of honor and respect by virtue of wisdom and experience, and I add the word *love* to that definition.

As the mother of two daughters, an advocate for women, and the founder of Venerable Women—an organization dedicated to the awakening of our highest selves, I have committed my personal and professional life to supporting venerable women. These dear souls have chosen to manifest a kind and loving world—starting within themselves. My personal vow is to work toward manifesting the Dalai Lama's vision of a saved, liberated, and elevated world, to live in that awareness myself, and to share what I learn along the way.

From my own experience and the wisdom of those I have coached and admired, and from a call out to the heavens to guide me that day in my kitchen, twelve attitudes for transformation emerged. I called them *Venerable Attitudes*. Once I shared them, women began calling them *V-Attitudes*.

The V-Attitudes described in this book are a proclamation, an inspiration, a practice, and a promise. With these guiding principles, let us begin. This intentional transformation journey, which we take together, provides fresh inspiration and new tools for living, leading to inner awareness and fulfillment of our needs and desires: expansion, growth, and clarity, as well as rich community. With love, honor, and respect for our shared journey, please join me in transforming ourselves and our world.

Part 1

A New Day

I wonder if my parents, Arthur and Vicky Morningstar, had any idea when they agreed to name me Dawn (Grandmother Rosie's suggestion), that my name would reaffirm my future passionate commitment to encouraging women (me included) to begin each day anew in the pursuit of our highest and best selves.

Childhood playmates made fun of my name. I appreciated that my teenage friends said it was "weird, but cool." When I introduce myself to new people, I sense a question on some faces that occasionally prompts me to add, "Yes, Dawn Morningstar is my real name."

The label that once caused me to avoid calling attention to it has become an apt symbol for my life's work.

Dawn is the first appearance of light before sunrise—after the dark of night. The word evokes the emergence from darkness into the comfort and inspiration of a new day with brand-new possibilities.

Such a dawning is possible not just each day, but in *each moment*. In our moment-by-moment choosing, we can rise up out of any darkness and have a fresh start. As we choose to let go of what *was* and create a new way of being, our enlightened choices result in better outcomes.

Called the morning star, Venus is the bright planet visible in the east just before sunrise. "Venus has a long history of association with the Divine Feminine," according to astrologer and energy worker, Emily Trinkaus, which goes as far back as the myth of Sumerian goddess, Inanna (meaning "Lady of Heaven") recorded on cuneiform tablets around 2500 BCE.[1]

Mary Magdalene is another representative of the Feminine Divine. After Christ's crucifixion, Mary Magdalene journeyed to the South of France and established her ministry. She was known as "Mary Lucifera" or "Mary the Light-bringer." To ancient Romans, *Lucifer* (Latin for "light-bringer") meant the morning star, or Venus—the one who brings forth Holy Light. Patriarchal religious leaders tried to change the connotations of the name to demean the powerful sacredness of the Feminine Divine by linking it with evil. For many, the name Lucifer now is associated with the devil or Satan.

Author Lynn Picknett explains, "Pagan goddesses were known, for example, as Diana Lucifera or Isis

---

1 *The Mountain Astrologer*, "Venus, Mary Magdalene, and the Re-emerging Sacred Feminine," 2015.

Lucifer to signify their power to illumine mind and soul... to open up both body and psyche to the Holy Light."[2]

As we awaken to the truth of women's value and worth, which is seeded in the Feminine Divine, we are inspired to proclaim our own personal transformations. We can begin anew as many times as it takes to become the women we came to this world to be. That is how it works for each of us. We awaken to the truth of who we really are and the profound impact we can make each day and in each moment.

We take our roles in history as the ones who transform the world in joyful and meaningful ways. In the words of the Hopi elder, "We are the ones we have been waiting for."

❧ ❧ ❧

My mother abandoned me when I was nine months old. She left me at my paternal grandmother Rosie's house one Saturday evening and never came back. Certainly, the sadness of those early years, and the subsequent knowledge that my mother *chose* not to be in my life, morphed into an unnamable feeling of unworthiness. Unworthiness wove itself into the very fabric of my being. Many years, tears, and discoveries cut the cloth, laid it onto a pattern, and was crafted into the attire I wore in my soul. But my story is only one of millions of stories, past and present

---

2 *The Secret History of Lucifer,* 2012.

and all over the world, that make up a huge photo mosaic made up of scenes from the lives of the feminine. If we were to look closely at the tiny photos making up the larger photo, we would see familiar patterns.

In some little pictures, infant girls are allowed to die or even caused to die because their lives were not seen as valuable as a boy child. In other tiny photos, we see girls sexually abused in incestuous behaviors beginning sometimes even in infancy. For many the abuse does not stop there, but becomes a pattern throughout their lives, during which they blame themselves somehow for the abuse and suffer more for that reason. Some photos reveal little girls being taught how to serve, give, and do for everyone else first, always first—at any cost.

Some tiny photos show girls sexualized by advertising and media and/or becoming anorexic as a way to exert some control over their lives—as comedian Margaret Cho (who struggles with her own eating disorders) put it, being skinny so as not to "take up too much space."

Other pictures illustrate teenage girls doing anything crude, rude, or nude to garner attention from a boy. Some of what happens is horrific and devaluing to both girls and boys. Some photos capture young women being sexually harassed at work or financially harassed by not being paid a fair and equal wage. Some photos show the well-hidden heartbreak of a young mother forced for financial reasons to leave her newborn and go back to work too soon or having to leave her older children to fend for themselves and each other.

Again and again, this photographic mosaic shows the sacred and loving natural wiring within women being cut away, and the resulting cords are scattered about like so much trash.

In one tiny photo within the larger sad montage of the feminine, my own mother's story is captured—the tale of being abandoned by her mother, and her mother's story of a cold and detached mother before that. My mother was one of five children born to a young Irish woman and a Sicilian immigrant. Grandfather Vittorio ran a fairly successful restaurant in Baltimore long before I was born. When he died unexpectedly, he left behind a young wife and five hungry children. Grandmother Mary had no way of knowing how to manage the Italian restaurant. Rather than giving away her children to relatives, which was frequently done in those days when hardship befell, my grandmother chose to keep her five offspring and do the only thing she knew how to do to feed, house, and clothe them. She remarried almost immediately.

The man Mary married was much younger than she. By most accounts he was a handsome but slippery kind of person who later wiggled himself into the beds of each of the children. My mother, Vicky, twelve years old at the time, barely escaped his centipede hands and twisted intent. Pictures reveal that my mother was a beautiful little girl with big brown eyes and uncontrollable shiny curls. Perhaps she was no more or less beautiful than any other child, for we know in the depth of our hearts that all children are beautiful and deserving of love and protection. But that was not to be in her childhood.

According to Vicky, when she told her mother about her stepfather's attempt to fondle her, Mary flew into a rage. Her rage bounced around the flowery wallpaper like lightning strikes pummeling a garden. The strikes were not aimed at her husband. Instead, the crashes landed jaggedly at the feet and heart of her trembling daughter.

"You must have done something to provoke it," Mary shot with the final bolt.

Almost immediately, Mary sent her bewildered daughter to an all-girls Catholic boarding school. The rest of Vicky's childhood was spent as a laborer in the school laundry, underfed and berated as a worthless sinner. She and the other young girls there were beaten when disobedient and sometimes whipped or given black eyes.

In these snapshots of a few generations of my own family in the larger mosaic of the feminine, I can see many patterns of loss, abandonment, and abuse. My healing task is to break the pattern in my family. Our shared healing task is to do the same in each family. The children are us—the ones to be protected, cherished, valued, taught to feel worthy, and who will influence the world for good. We do not have to literally have our own children to continue our personal family lineage; for some, that is not a possibility or a choice. However, as women, we are the ones who, when honored and loved, will be better equipped to protect, love, and cherish others in relationships of all sorts and, as role models, transform the future for our daughters, sisters, mothers, aunts, cousins, and friends—by healing ourselves.

We can be sure that no one who is loved, happy, fulfilled, and valued will intentionally inflict injury on others. Our hurts reflect what came before us even when we are not aware of the specific details or the people. We are the middle bridge between the generations long gone and those yet to be born. If we visualize all we have inherited as a treasure chest, whether known or not yet discovered, we can see things that need polishing, cleaning, repair, and renewal. We can take responsibility for creating that renewal and become the needed blessing. Our healing and transformation raise the vibrational energy of all life—past, present, and future. With awareness, courage, and acceptance, we take new and beautiful photos for the mosaic that tells the recreated stories of our lives.

PART II
FULL CIRCLE

S poken and unspoken directives are given to many girl children from a society and culture when its masculine and feminine are far out of balance.

Don't expect too much.
Give to others first.
Everyone and everything is more important than what you want.
Be humble and be quiet.
You are not worthy and should be happy with what you get.
Your value comes from how you look.

These messages translate into an internal dialogue that is challenging to counter. Patriarchy has ruled for so long and so deeply that a distortion and devaluation of feminine attributes has become commonplace as part of a shared consciousness. This mind-set serves no one.

❖ ❖ ❖

Seeds of unworthiness were planted, watered, and took deep root in the first few formative years of my own life. Feeling undeserving of love, honor, and respect colored everything I was and did for many years. After being passed from family member to family member multiple times in my first year of life, my baby clothes, diapers, and bottles packed into cardboard boxes, someone finally kept me. My father's mother, Rosie McNulty, said "yes" with her heart and with her actions. She was a gracious soul who everyone loved—especially me. My Rosie, whom I called Mom Mom (pronounced *mum mum*) was my dearest love. She vowed to raise me as her own child, and she did.

As a little girl, I asked Mom Mom where my mother was and why she didn't come to see me. Rosie never told me that my mother lived and worked less than ten miles away. Instead she answered my question by taking out the yellowing Polaroid photo of my parents on their wedding day and pointing to my mother.

"Dawnie, this is your mom, Vicky. She loves you very much. Isn't she beautiful?"

With a smile that did not match the sadness in her eyes, Rosie would place the photo back in the wooden engraved box, change the subject, and ask me if I wanted a special snack. On some days, when the look in Rosie's eyes was especially sad, she told me to go play outside for a while. And I did.

As years passed, I agonized about why I didn't have a mom like my school friends and that no one would tell me why. I thought that I must have been a bad baby or unlovable or that there was something horribly wrong with me for my own mother to leave me and never come back. When kids at school asked me where my mother was, I fabricated amazing stories.

I answered, "My mother? Oh, she died when I was little," or, "She's a very important businesswoman who lives in France." Or sometimes perhaps, I offered, "She couldn't be here today, but maybe next time." Some days I came home from school and cried.

My mother's much-younger sister, Mary, came to visit me from time to time. I was so grateful and felt tremendous excitement whenever I knew she was coming. Mary looked so much like my mom in the photo Rosie showed me that I sometimes pretended Mary *was* my mom.

I adored Auntie Mary's playful spirit. We played board games and ate giant ice cream cones. I loved Mary so much. She seemed like an angel to me. When I looked in her dark-brown eyes, I saw something familiar that I could not describe.

One April day in 1973, I was devastated to learn that my Mary, just twenty-five years old, was killed in a car accident. This beautiful, sparkling, loving, young woman was gone. My pain ran deep. Not only was my mom gone, but so also was my only connection to her. Mary's love for me had become a soothing balm to my wounded heart.

I was jarred from my thoughts of Mary and all she meant to me when my father asked if I was going to the funeral home. Without thinking, and through tears, I quickly said, "Of course."

He invited me to consider it carefully because, "Dawnie, your mother will be there."

Questions raced back and forth in my mind: *Am I ready to meet her? What will she be like? Will she like me? Will she ignore me? What should I wear?*

I was sixteen years old and had not seen my mother in almost sixteen years. I did not know what she looked like in real life. I had only seen her smiling in what I imagined to be red lipstick in the faded black-and-white Polaroid from all those years ago.

I prayed long that night for answers and guidance. Though I had prayed many times as a girl, those prayers were usually for things, such as: *Please God, bring me a Barbie doll house, have Mom Mom make spaghetti and meatballs for dinner, or let that cute boy notice me on the bus.* My prayers on this night were very different. That my whole life could be greatly changed based on the decision I made wasn't lost on me. I did not know exactly how, but my decision could have huge consequences.

I cried quietly in my bedroom and continued to beg God for an answer. If I did go to meet my mother, would she accept me and not turn away, or would she break my heart? *Please, Mom, not again.*

My decision whether or not to meet my mother might even impact my dear Rosie. *Might Rosie think that doing so meant I was not grateful to her for all she had done in my mother's absence? Who would I think of as my mother? Vicky? Rosie?* I felt so confused.

After spending all night kneeling, pacing the room, climbing on and off the bed, tossing and turning, and trying to fall asleep, I finally felt the presence of my Divine. It was not like in the movies, some thunderous voice booming from a ray of golden light in the heavens. There was no voice really, and no words, yet the answer was clear.

The next evening, I walked into the funeral home wearing a borrowed blue dress (nicer than any dress I owned) that began to feel damp in its folds. I scanned the room and saw many mourners, all bearing the weight of shock and profound sorrow at the loss of Mary, such a beautiful and shining soul.

There, next to my dear Aunt Mary's coffin, stood a woman. This woman, dark-haired and petite, bent over Aunt Mary's body like the tender branch of a weeping willow. She cried so hard, yet so silently, that she shook. My knees began to match the rhythm of her shaking. I noticed that my palms were wet and so were my cheeks. I wiped away one of many tears that came that evening.

This woman was my mom in the flesh, the woman I had wondered about and missed all my life. She was standing within a few feet of me.

Without thinking, I walked up to her and felt a flood of emotions. I heard the words tumble out of my mouth, "Hi Mom, I'm Dawn," and I hugged her.

She hugged me back, hard and for a long time. Many of the mourners in the funeral home knew the two of us had been apart all those years and were filled with emotion at the sight of us hugging and crying. My mother and I both cried—for the loss of Mary and for the joy of two of us being together again.

That evening, my mother, father, and I went to dinner. Sitting at the table together, sharing stories of our lives, and having a delicious meal in a fancy restaurant seemed dreamlike. I had pondered what my mother would be like my entire life. And here she was, beautiful and funny, her expressive chocolate-brown eyes smiling at me across the table as though this was something the three of us had done all along.

A few months later, my mother and father married each other again after all of those years divorced. They remained married for more than four decades until Dad's death in 2007. Mom died one year later.

❧ ❧ ❧

In the years before I went to meet my mother at the funeral home, my life was sweet in many ways that counterbalanced the longing for my mother and intermittent contact with my father. Aunt Joan, Rosie's daughter, was sixteen years old when I came to live with them and was soon to be married and moving away. After that, my Rosie and I lived a quiet life, a little girl and her grandmother.

Rosie was born at the turn of the twentieth century. She spoke to me like an adult and taught me to be polite and thoughtful. She dressed me in frilly dresses, crinolines, lace-trimmed socks, little white gloves, and bonnets—nothing like the current fashion trends in the 1960s. Rosie's old-fashioned ways were challenging for me at times. School friends made fun of my clothes.

I was different in other ways too. I spent a lot of time alone. I was enthralled with the stained-glass windows and rituals of the Catholic Church where Rosie took me every Sunday morning. I considered angels and saints as my friends. I talked to them and invited the Blessed Mother to my tea parties. I loved to pray and pretended my bedroom was a church or a convent.

Rosie cooked all our meals from scratch and joked that she spent so much time in the kitchen she would probably die there. She planted Maryland tomatoes in our garden; we picked the plumpest ones and ate them outside while they were still warm from the summer sun.

When I was in my early teens, Rosie used to say, "I just want to live long enough to see you grown and independent."

The morning after my senior prom, and one week before I graduated high school in 1975, Rosie died of a heart attack in her kitchen, illustrating the power of her two proclamations, dying in her kitchen and living long enough to see me grown.

I am forever grateful for the woman who said yes to loving me and raising me as her own child just like she said she would.

❧ ❧ ❧

After finally meeting my mom and then after years of internal work with the help of counseling, prayer, meditation, and every other self-improvement and spiritual pursuit I could find, including becoming a professional coach, I wondered why I didn't feel better than I did. I looked happy on the outside, and certainly was at times, yet there was pain that continued to keep me from who I wanted to be. Why did my spiritual practices work sometimes and not at others? How was I still attracting and maintaining situations that were not in my own best interests? Why did I attract and stay too long in toxic relationships? There was still something missing. I really wanted to find out what it was—for myself, for my dear daughters, my friends, my growing clientele, for all humanity really—and on behalf of my mother.

Some might think, and a few people actually said at the time, that reuniting with my mother at Aunt Mary's funeral and my parents then coming back together should have healed me. After all, "You had a wonderful grandmother raise you, you had food and shelter, and now your family is back together."

But what I heard asked by others and murmured in my own mind then and for years to come were the questions, *What more could you want? Why are you unhappy? Why do you still feel bad about yourself?*

My deeply ingrained unworthiness whispered and sometimes shouted. Blasphemous negative messaging, corded to my soul, caused me over many years to make poor choices in every area—relationships, lifestyle, and profession. *You're not good enough. You are not enough. Even your own mother didn't want you. You are not good.* I felt unworthy of love, honor, and respect—and my decisions in life reflected that clearly.

❧ ❧ ❧

My mother and I navigated our way through the murky waters of our wounded souls. We loved each other for sure, yet avoided the hard conversations, the authentic truths that could have healed us both, sooner and deeper. Avoidance of our suffering brought us more suffering.

When I was married, with two daughters, and living in Minnesota, 1,200 miles away from my mother, our visits entailed marathon conversations, sometimes long into the night. My parents' home in Baltimore had a side deck made of aged gray wood with a black wrought-iron table and three chairs.

When we first arrived at my parents' home and everyone reunited, Mom and Dad would catch up on the latest with the girls, Lauren and Lindsay, and usually shower them with gifts. We ate my mother's Maryland crab cakes, lovingly made from her secret recipe. After dishes were washed and the girls played with their new loot on the floor at their grandfather's feet, Mom and I retreated to the side deck. The kids understood that the only reason to interrupt us was if there was some kind of emergency—which did not include losing a Barbie shoe or running out of cookies. Mom brought out her mother's beautiful Italian wine glasses, and they bore witness throughout the night to our stories, secrets, and dreams.

Over the years, our talks went back to the topic of my mother's and my own "soul contract" (as I came to think of it). That pre-birth soul agreement from my perspective included my abandonment as a baby, being raised by a loving grandmother, our family reuniting when I was a teenager, and performing the "dance" between my mother and I that continued, accompanied by music of our own making. In this dance, we repeated the steps of telling the story from her perspective and then from mine, though the word "abandonment" did not make it to the dance floor. Instead, Abandonment, dressed in its dull and constant shade of pain, sat watching, waiting, and witnessing both of us.

Toward the end of her life, Mom finally filled in what had previously been a sketchy story about her life and her mother's. Grandmother Mary had been sent away as a small child to live with a cruel aunt. *Abandonment.* Mom filled in more details about the cruelty of the nuns who were indifferent to her pain when Grandmother Mary sent her away. *Abandonment.* Mom had climbed over the wall of the school and escaped at age sixteen. Only weeks later, she met my father and married him almost immediately. Mom told of her initial joy in marrying my dad and having a baby girl. But then she told of her fear, sadness, and anger when Dad began gambling, drinking, womanizing, and leaving her alone with an infant and no money. *Abandonment.* She talked about her fear while trying to figure out how to make a living as a woman with only a high school education in the 1950s, without support from family, and with no self-esteem.

Mom poured another glass of wine, invited Abandonment onto the dance floor, and cranked up the music. She spoke of the pain of working in a local pub as a bartender and trying to figure out what to do with her baby. She described her confusion and guilt as she passed me from family member to family member until finally my grandmother, Rosie, said "yes" and took me in.

Mom talked about the many times she came to visit me. Tears welled in her eyes as she said how my baby cries for her to come back when she was leaving followed her down the sidewalk, through her car window, and into her dreams for days to come. *Abandonment.* Vicky Morningstar had no way to deal with the pain she felt hearing her baby cry for her when she left Rosie's house or the cries whenever she took me from Rosie's arms. So my mother decided one day she could never come back. *Abandonment.*

The song stopped playing, Abandonment took her seat and was glad she had been brought to the dance floor. My mother and I looked at each other with knowing eyes and decided it was time to ask Compassion onto the dance floor.

❧ ❧ ❧

When I found out Mom had less than a year to live, I moved from my home of twenty years in Minnesota back to Maryland to take care of her. Dad died the year before and the two of them had lived in Baltimore all their lives. Though I hoped to take care of Mom at my home in Minnesota, she understandably wanted to be around people and places familiar to her. I cared for her twenty-four hours a day, seven days a week, for nine months until she left this earth.

Moving back to Baltimore was a hard decision because it meant leaving my seventeen-year-old daughter, Lindsay, back in Minnesota to finish her senior year of high school. My heart ached leaving Lindsay, but she understood and supported the decision. She knew her grandmother needed me.

Late one afternoon as light streamed through the floral sheer curtains my mother loved, I held her frail body next to me and stroked her head, bald from chemotherapy. I felt a tender love for this woman whose lack of love, honor, and respect from others in her life caused her deep pain.

Though Mom could barely speak, she described how one night when I was a baby, she was exhausted after a long work shift at the bar. She came at 3:30 in the morning to pick me up from one of the many locations she left me in those days. She found me sitting in a filthy playpen, dirty, hungry, wet, and crying. In that moment, she imagined herself as a young child and vowed she would never raise her daughter like that. She believed that if Rosie, my dad's mom, would say yes to taking care of me, I would have a good life. She said, "I wanted better for you."

Mom said she cried each day she was away from me. Her eyes misted over as she said that when I walked into the funeral home in the borrowed blue dress and back into her life, "You gave me a miracle that day, Dawnie."

We both cried and held each other as the light through the curtains began to dim, and night fell silently and kindly.

For nine months, the same amount of time as a human pregnancy, I bathed my mom, took her to doctors' appointments, and picked up her prescription medications. I coordinated oxygen tank deliveries and pickups, grocery shopped, cleaned, cooked, and tucked her into bed every night. Having never been trained in Reiki, I did my own version on Mom's tiny back to help relieve the pain caused by radiation treatments. I held my hands a few inches above the painful areas of her body and prayed for healing, soothing energy to flow through me into her. Mom would smile and say she felt better. That made me happier than I can say.

For the most part toward the end of her life, Mom was rarely able to go out of the house. One day I asked her if she would like to visit her favorite vacation spot in Ocean City, Maryland, one last time, where our family had gone for years. She said, "Oh, Dawnie, I would love that."

I rented a big house on the bay near the ocean and invited family members and a few friends to come stay with us. We knew this would be Mom's last time in her beloved Ocean City, and we all wanted to share that experience with her. I tend to have a Norman Rockwell vision of how visits and holidays come about and, though we had a few hiccups with fourteen people people, all in all, it was lovely.

On the three-hour drive home, Mom said from the back seat of the car, which we made up like a little bed, "That was the best trip I ever had." She could not stop saying thank you. Mom was thanking me and, I believe, she was thanking the ocean, the sky, the sand, the air, and her God.

One day after we returned to her home, Mom became very weak. I made up her bed with a ton of pillows and placed fresh flowers on her nightstand. To complete the effect of a fancy hotel, I placed a chocolate on her pillow. When it came time for her to go to bed, Mom walked slowly into her room with me a few steps behind, which had become our habit in case she stumbled or began to fall. She saw the room, the flowers, and the pillows, and then her eyes landed on the piece of chocolate wrapped in gold foil. I will never forget the look she had on her face in that moment or the hug she gave me. As weak as she was, her strong hug almost took my breath away. I felt a powerful blessing fill that room, and I believe Mom did too.

Each day thereafter we looked for fun and meaningful things to do—talking about her life, my life, watching movies on TV, following politics (Mom loved politics and it was a presidential election year), and she finally shared the secret recipes for her famous Maryland crab cakes and "Vicky's Italian Meatballs."

Though Mom's appetite disappeared a little more each day, I cooked for her, sometimes making several different foods in a day, trying to land on something she could eat or would like to eat. On one moment that stands out among our final days together, I had prepared a tiny meal for her, some mashed potatoes with butter and sour cream, just the way she liked them—alongside a little creamed corn. Mom was very weak and had a hard time sitting up. I wrapped one arm around her shoulders and offered my sweet appreciative mother, so tiny now, small, soft bites. The feeling of holding her, rocking her gently when the pain cut through her, and feeding her with a child-size spoon, made me realize that she and I had come full circle. I was caring for her as a mother would care for her baby. I felt that love, honor, and respect were restored to us each in that moment. I loved her truly and deeply and knew she loved me too. Then she was gone.

My soul contract and life experience with Vicky Morningstar set me on a path in search of worthiness that inspired my life's work.

Part iii

Lessons Along the Path to Venerable

The story of the life of Mary Magdalene is a compelling one. At one point, I believed myself to be a reincarnation of Mary Magdalene. I really did.

When I was a teenager in the 1970s, *Jesus Christ Superstar* burst onto the theater scene in Baltimore. I sat in a cushy red velvet seat and was moved beyond reason when I heard the song *I Don't Know How to Love Him*. Hearing it sung in the cavernous theater, I felt tears running down my face. I just *knew* that I had been Mary Magdalene in a past life. Surely I would have been the kind of woman who would stand beside a man like Jesus and support his teachings to inspire the expansion of love of self and others—and oneness with the Divine. I had a tender spot for this Jesus, not so much as a man when I really thought about it, but as a great teacher who offered a brand new paradigm for humanity based solely on love.

I offer my apologies in advance to those not as chock full of Catholicism as I, for going down this path. The lessons from the Catholic Church poured into me as a child and informed much of my early spirituality. Yet I invite you along this side road for a reason. Along the way, we see example after example of women in history being portrayed as anything but venerable.

I was raised Catholic and attended Catholic school through twelfth grade, ending up at an all-girls Catholic high school. Girls were sent either because they were pious, they were bright, their parents wanted a fine education for them or, in many cases, this was a last hope to straighten out these girls' lives once and for all.

My classmates at The Catholic High School fit into all those categories. I believe I was sent there for the fine education, and I was mostly naïve about the ones who were there as a last hope. The last-hope girls were drinking, drugging, and having sex. Though I drank my fair share of Boone's Farm and Singapore Slings, I did not even know what the girls were talking about when it came to sex and drugs.

In our classrooms, crosses hung everywhere to remind us of Christ's suffering and death on our behalf. There was no escape. Teachings about God, the afterlife, this life, what women should and should not do, sex (don't have it unless you are pleasing your husband or trying to conceive), and sins (some could condemn you to eternal damnation) were force-fed to me, my fellow students, and throngs of followers of the Church. The teachings and dogma were never allowed to be questioned or discussed—even when we intuitively felt something false in our gut.

Much earlier, as a little girl in Catechism classes on Sunday mornings before church, I asked sincere questions about how if God created everything and was everything, everywhere, omnipresent—does that mean God was in hell, too? Did he go there and comfort people in hell, because they must have been suffering and sad, burning in flames like that and all, right? Or, if God loved his creations so very much, why did he condemn some of them to spend all eternity there in the first place? Why was God a man?

Later as a teenager, I questioned why there were no women priests. If I wanted to serve the Divine in a religious capacity (which I truly did in those days and even considered becoming a nun), would it have to be as a nun and never in a leadership role like priests, bishops, or the pope, authorities in our church?

The responses were always the same whether from my Sunday school teacher, nuns who taught me, or priests who occasionally gave instruction in grade school. "That is the way it is, and you do not question it at all, ever, or you will be sinning against God, Dawn Morningstar."

The teachings in many organized religions are immutable and designed to trump an individual's personal experience of the Divine—keeping religion as the unrelenting, judgmental, fickle, and ultimately controlling and cruel gatekeeper. "Religion knows best" is the creed, similar in feeling to the idea that Father Knows Best. But really, did father always know best?

❧ ❧ ❧

Through the years, long after my Catholic school teachings and questioning, I met more and more women on the spiritual path. Sometimes after we meditated or prayed, drank a glass of wine, or had a discussion about Mary Magdalene or Jesus being married, a woman in the group would state with certainty that *she* had been Mary Magdalene in a past life! This actually happened fairly often! I reasoned that, since we could not all have been Mary Magdelenes, there must have been a reason so many women strongly and intuitively believed it was true.

Is it really any wonder that we may have felt that Mary Magdalene, as the wife and lover of Christ—his close companion, cherished friend, colleague, fellow spiritual leader, and one held in great respect by him, was the woman we longed to be? Mary Magdalene's brilliance and stature and archetypal energy, as a loved, honored, and respected woman, give her a place in human history that few women occupy.

Perhaps we are drawn to the idea of experiencing Divine sexuality with the "perfect" God/man? That Mary Magdalene was portrayed as a prostitute is surely one of the many ways she and countless other women have been diminished, misrepresented, or not represented at all in our literature, teachings, art, and stories.

I presumed that because Jesus lived when he did, his culture would demand he marry. Though commonly held that Jesus spoke Aramaic, there was no word for *bachelor* in the Hebrew language in the first century AD. Then consider the story in The Gospel according to John in which Mary, the mother of Jesus, speaks with authority that the wine is running low at a wedding feast at Cana. A woman like Mary would have had no authority or voice in those days about such matters at a wedding unless the wedding was for one of her own children. Was the wedding at Cana her son Jesus's for her to speak with such authority?

After being initially shocked at such proposed heresy, Roman Catholic scholar and university instructor, Margaret Starbird, author of *The Woman With the Alabaster Jar,* set out to refute the idea that Jesus was married. So compelled and convinced by her research, Starbird arrived at the *opposite* conclusion—deciding that Jesus had, in fact, been married. She concluded that Mary Magdalene *was* his wife.

Starbird convincingly presents the question and then answers it logically, referring to the Bible passages when rare and expensive oils anoint Jesus' feet.

"...there came a woman with an alabaster jar of ointment, genuine nard of great value; and breaking the alabaster jar, she poured it on his head." ~Mark 14:3 (ESV)

Then Mary took a pound of ointment, genuine nard of great value, and anointed the feet of Jesus and wiped his feet dry with her hair. And the house was filled with the fragrance of her ointment." ~John 12:3 (NIV)

Starbird asks, "Who is doing that?" Mary Magdalene is. Who else would have access to those oils? Only a woman who was a high priestess—or the woman anointing the feet of her bridegroom would. In either case, she was a woman of high stature, not a prostitute.

While on the topic of prostitution and sex, consider how what we think about sex influences the way we think of women overall. The mother of Christ supposedly did not have sex to conceive him. Neither apparently was her son thought to have sexual relations with anyone. The Catholic Church's priests and nuns are required to be celibate and not engage in what is most natural and necessary to the sensual encounter of humanity.

For some, celibacy can be a choice to commune with the Divine in purity and devotion. But the history of the Catholic Church, including sexual relations between priests and nuns (and others outside the church) and widespread childhood sexual abuse, reveals some onerous issues and outcomes related to sex and celibacy. How might this change for the better if the Catholic Church were to include women as respected and equal partners in leadership? And how would other world religions be elevated if they too embraced the attributes of the Feminine Divine, honoring all of life?

Emily Trinkaus, professional astrologer and energy worker, invites us to consider this: "Can we all just pause for a moment and imagine what adolescence would have been like, what our intimate relationships and sex lives would be like, what our relationship with our own bodies would be like, and what the whole freakin' world would be like, if we'd grown up with a sexual Jesus, a lover of women? With a Mary Magdalene who was Jesus's spiritual equal and partner in sacred sexuality? With a Mother Mary whose 'divine birth' of Jesus had nothing to do with chastity and everything to do with the sacredness of ALL life, as if the ability to create another human in one's body were a divine miracle in and of itself?"[3]

The perception of sex as sacred lies buried deep in the psyche of both men and women. Healthy sexuality, with women (and men) as sacred participants does much to further our sense of worthiness and positively impacts our sexual partners as well. Yet the more common misrepresentations of sex as impure and sinful outside of marriage and procreation impact each of us in insidious ways. The alchemy of masculine and feminine attributes has a

---

3 "Crucify the Old Stories, Resurrect Your Divine Body: the Peak of the Cardinal Grand Cross, Venus in Pisces, and the Grand Water Trine," April 2014. See http://virgomagic.com/2014/04/cardinal-cross-2014/.

definite resonance. Both are necessary and at their best when expressed, valued, and united.

The movie, *Pretty Woman*, is both revered and reviled. Julia Roberts, playing the role of a prostitute, uses her sexuality, sensuality, and personality to make a living and ultimately finds true love with one of her johns. He happens to be handsome, well accomplished, and rich. A message of the film is the trading of feminine sensuality and sexuality for money.

Though a woman should have the freedom to do with her body as she pleases, the primary problem with prostitution and sexual abuse is the imbalance of power—whether given away or taken away. If women had other resources, how many would choose prostitution? When a woman's sensuality comes from a deep part within her in an expression and extension of love, nurturance, compassion, connection, and beauty, there is not much on this earth lovelier to experience or receive.

Turning our attention back to Mary Magdalene—whether she is portrayed as a whore or a high priestess *should* concern us. How else have women been wrongly portrayed or not portrayed at all in our history books, in our teachings, in our psyches? These omissions or misrepresentations matter.

Who would condone little girls to be costumed as witches wearing pointed black hats for Halloween if we understood what implications lie underneath the portrayal of witches? In 1400s Europe, noble women

of the upper classes wore tall conical hats called hennins. Like many fashion trends, it took a while for
styles to catch up in outlying villages; after they went
out of vogue, hennins would no longer be seen in royal
courts and wealthy circles, but would make their way
to villages and towns and be worn by women there.
At about the same time, the Church was trying to
replace Paganism (the old religion) with Christianity
(the new religion). One of many ways the Church did
this was to declare that the point of a woman's hat
represented the devil's horns and, by association,
the women still practicing the old religion who wore
them were evil.[4] We honor women more if we were
to costume our daughters and granddaughters as
goddesses, leaders, or powerful women at Halloween
instead of the bastardized version of witches we have
been programmed to believe in.

The Burning Times, a 1990 Canadian documen-
tary, which presents a feminist account of the Early
Modern European witchcraft trials, estimates that
nine million women (yes, 9,000,000) were accused
of and killed for being witches. Many history
books cite much lower numbers. What does your
own intuition tell you about this? Killing millions
of women is quite an effective way to silence their
voices. Women's knowledge of healing, birthing,
history, stories, wisdom, traditions and rituals, their

---

4 *The Witch Book: The Encyclopedia of Witchcraft, Wicca, and
Neo-paganism* by Raymond Buckland. Visible Ink Press,
2002.

fortunes, and their lives were extinguished. An evil form of patriarchy stole their voices, their property, their power, and their perpetuity.

This quote from *Malleus Malificatum* (witch hammer) in 1486 is an example of the beliefs about women in those times: "If we inquire, we find that all the kingdoms of the world have been overthrown by women."

Fast forward to the twenty-first century where we see many examples of women being overlooked and devalued for their contributions from those ancient times until now. Who is likely to be credited for the huge biological discovery of the twenty-third set of chromosomes, X and Y? Most textbooks point to a man named Thomas Morgan, but the discovery actually was made by a female scientist, Nettie Stevens. Volumes could be written about women who were not credited or, in some cases, not even mentioned for their contributions.

No wonder so many women still feel a need to stay quiet about certain topics, and not see how glorious, valuable, and worthy we truly are. We remember someplace deep down in our cellular memory that to speak out, to play with big heart in the world, to lead, or to offer gentler, more loving ways of being (like our fifteenth century sisters did when they practiced Paganism, which venerated nature and honored the many faces of the Feminine Divine) will not necessarily be valued or welcomed. Instead we have known disrespect, diminishment, torture, and had our tongues literally cut out. From

what well will we find the waters of courage to succeed, speak our minds, and stand in our power?
What price may we still have to pay—even in these
"enlightened" times?

At this very moment, women are called to
awaken, yet again, to their rightful place on this
earth. This time though, we can do it *together* as
worthy, self-actualized beings. We do not right past
wrongs by imitating past persecutors and detractors.
Neither is it our intent to harm males in our lives or
to claim power *over* them. Power serves best when it
is *within* and when we collaborate, cooperate, and
empower others.

❧ ❧ ❧

What is our path? Where are the nourishing bread-
crumbs that will lead us to communion with the
highest possible version of ourselves? I sought such
crumbs and placed those I found in the basket of
my consciousness to practice and share with my sisters. And one day, instead of crumbs in my basket, I
found a loaf!

While sitting across from a spiritual healer many
years ago in a warm glow of candles lit and flickering, I was asked if I wanted to do a past life regres-
sion or deep meditation. I chose deep meditation
because, at that time, I was not sure about the value
in knowing of past lives or if I wanted to know about
them at all. What good could it do? Was that really
a *thing*?

While in guided deep meditation, however, past lives began appearing anyway, one after another in rapid pace, bouncing around from the present day to the past. Images from my former lives flashed before me—one lifetime as a strong hairy man wearing animal skins, one as a small, pale, sickly child, another as a cave-dwelling woman with a pregnant belly, a noblewoman during the French Revolution about to be beheaded for standing with the people, a beggar boy with twisted limbs, as a woman I believed to be Mary Magdalene (a high priestess, not a prostitute), and one as a weathered Aborigine elder sitting perched in a tree, scanning the horizon for something in the distance.

What felt like an early, or maybe first, lifetime come into surprising focus with great detail unlike the glimpses of lifetimes past that were fleeting and without much specificity. I saw myself in a simple robe sitting on a marble bench engraved with sacred geometric symbols. Around me were women I instinctively knew were in an ethereal place of the Feminine Divine. We learned from one another, sharing ancient and contemporary teachings and wisdom, healing, inner knowing, traditions, inspiration, and stories. Each woman embodied the essence of her most loving feminine self—and was treasured for her work on behalf of humanity. We had made commitments to do this work in ways best suited to our individual gifts and talents. We were in all ways abundant—in riches, relationships, and fulfillment. My role was to hold sacred space in the temple. As a host and inspirer, I welcomed and connected the women when they arrived.

A plaque, which could only be read with the eyes of a kind heart, hovered in the air beside the arched portal. Letters of living vines with green leaves spelled out the words Temple of Venerable Women. No matter how many times their feet crossed the time-polished threshold, the women felt delighted and affirmed anew. Because the filigree platinum door only opened when a woman resonated with vibrations of love, peace, kindness, and joy, it required no lock. If the door did not open immediately, one of the Venerables came to listen, offer support, and remind the visitor of her truest self. Then the door opened as usual.

Inside the temple, the spectrum of light faceting the generous courtyard appeared other-worldly, as colors do in vivid dreams. A reverie of fine flowers and flickers on wicks floated on top sheets of water in shimmering pools. Women sat in sacred circles wearing chakra-colored flowing robes, billowing pants, or gossamer gowns.

The visiting sea breeze took holiday on the skin of each woman's face, neck, hands, and feet and knew just the right time to leave. The energies of the emerald sea in the east, violet mountains in the north, gold-dusted prairie in the west, and mossy hills in the south were the temple's outer walls. The inner walls kept confidences and stories.

Women inside spoke the wisdom of ancient inner knowing, reminding each other of the ways of venerable women. When younger women, *vebblewims* (so named by little girls who had trouble pronouncing "venerable women"), returned after having been there as girls under the age of twelve, they were inspired to draw out their knowledge of past teachings. Sessions included a fine-tuning and trusting of their inner wisdom, remembering the twelve paths of life as a venerable woman, self-awareness practices, and more. When a young venerable woman recited the teachings, she was celebrated with heart hugs, singing, basil honey drops, and a new gossamer gown. If her remembering was especially good, new shoes were placed upon her feet. Venerable women of any age love shoes.

Chortling from women, as they do when men are not around, allied with the rich sound of wooden chimes and harps. This unexpected symphony did not reach across the sun-dappled terrace where silent reflection was agreed upon. On the quiet terrace, the robed, gowned, and billow-panted appeared and disappeared around luminescent pillars which rose high into mist clouds colored lavender and spring green.

As widely known and understood, each person had a unique gift purpose that manifested when one took a first breath. Each one's gift purpose was decided before their conception while she or he was in the Knowing Time, wrapped in the arms of the Divine. Gifted, empowered, whole, and unfamiliar with shame or unworthiness, people honored their uniqueness and lived their true purposes.

Some chose the gift purpose to heal using their hands, practicing first on small birds with cracked wings. Some venerables held a holy space for the dying as they passed to the other side and transitioned to their next gift purpose. Some chose the art of procuring plants to make sacred and beneficial oils, and some committed to holding the space for beauty and creativity. Some gift purposes did not have a name, yet a woman knew she was on track because she felt alive with passion and intention. There were as many gift purposes as grains of sand, and each one loved what she or he offered the world.

Surprisingly, there was little mention of God, Source, Spirit, or the Divine. Everyone simply expressed as the essence of the I AM in words and deeds. They spent time in the Silence though, quieting their minds, listening and knowing Oneness with all.

The vebblewims grew into venerable women and continued to gather in the temple to remember, reawaken, practice, share, and support. When anyone teased that venerable women came to the temple only to rest and rejuvenate—that just made them laugh. The women were easily energized with good balance and boundaries in the outside world. They had committed their lives to make manifest a kind and loving world—in the ways only they, as venerable women, could do. "Love, honor, and respect" was the mantra of their being and the pulse in their veins.

The women were rightfully paid abundant sums of platinum, salt, and herbs as currency. They lived richly, attracting all their imaginations could conjure—and delighting in giving generously to others. Feeling dearly valued for their sacred work, they felt immense gratitude for their honored roles.

Women came to the temple at various times in their lives and then returned to the world they loved—to practice, serve, and delight. To say men and women respected one another was not a topic in circles of any kind because how else could it be?

Men were equally honored and respected for their sacred roles. Everyone's energy field blessed all people, places, and things. No armies were required, and there was no word for war. The birth of every baby was celebrated with great joy. All born were inherently good and it was the job of the community to help children to remember that about themselves.

As commonly understood and joyfully agreed upon, all venerables were cared for with love and compassion in their last days and left this earth with dignity and respect for their very being—because that is what they embodied and inspired in others.

⚜ ⚜ ⚜

Can you imagine yourself as one of the women in a place like the one I described? Can you imagine any place where every woman is giving and receiving love, honor, and respect? Perhaps you have already visited such a place. Perhaps it is not a place at all, but a state of being. We can come and go in our own versions of the Temple of Venerable Women at any time. Such is our birthright.

⚜ ⚜ ⚜

Our world faces huge challenges; poverty, hunger, income inequality, lack of education, war, hate, crime, disease, and hopelessness are only a handful. Many problems are solved when virtue and humanity's highest expressions of character reign. Women are wired to love and respect others and, as we grow in confidence, we use these attributes—and everything improves.

Because women are very good at tending to the needs of others with their own needs coming in a distant last, women need to be reawakened to our own power in order to do the work we came to this earth to do. We need to be peace-filled in order to promote peace, we must love ourselves in order to love the world, and we must have water in our well in order to quench the thirst of others. When we try to give from a place out of the fear that saying "no" can bring, depletion and exhaustion occur. When acknowledged, inspired, and supported, we love, serve, heal, and help more. When women and girls do better, so do their families, businesses, and communities. By bolstering girls and women to feel whole and healthy, we *can* be the change the Dalai Lama believes Western women are here to make. In addition to saving the world, women and girls will enjoy delightful lives—a win-win.

❧ ❧ ❧

Imagine what it will be like to be alive in a world of love, honor, respect, peace, collaboration, equality, prosperity, kindness, possibility, and joy—for all humans, for all living things. Go beyond visioning it, use all your senses to *feel* it—as though it is already happening. Imagining even the smallest details, as if they were already true, sets the conditions in place that we want to manifest.

❧ ❧ ❧

After receiving life coaching, I discovered that life coaching is my calling, too. I became a master certified coach (MCC) and began my private practice. Initially, my practice did not have a particular focus or specialty, but I was enthusiastic and dedicated. I wanted to coach absolutely everyone on everything because of my own positive experience, and I could see how this honoring service benefited others.

My client schedule was filled with men and women, and I coached them in a wide range of areas: a male fashion designer who wanted to learn to be a better businessperson, an accomplished woman executive whose secret dream was to be a published author of novels, a woman wanting to lose weight and become more fit, a minister approaching retirement who wanted to learn better leadership skills as she left her church, a woman on a board of directors of a national environmental organization who wanted to learn how to give an empowered speech, and a mature man who wanted to learn how to woo back his high school sweetheart. Others came because they had gone as far as they could on their own and felt stuck.

As years passed, I felt immense gratitude for the role I was honored with, supporting and witnessing each person's transformation. I grew more as a result of coaching others and began to ask myself some important questions.

How can I serve at the highest possible level?

In whose lives could I make the most difference?

Who could I coach who would create the most positive changes in the world? And as important, who did I *love* coaching the most and why?

The answer to all of the questions was the same. I *love* working with women. More specifically, I love working with women who are spiritually awake, self-aware, and know they are on this earth to manifest a kind and loving world. I saw myself in that group, too.

Some of the issues my women clients described:

- Unhealthy relationships with family members, friends, significant others
- Poor or no boundaries
- Debilitating negative self-talk
- Fear of becoming a bag lady (even from women with wealth)
- The need to give to others without regard for self needs

- Perfectionism—in order to be loved
- Worries about the future/locked in the past
- A sense of disconnection from the Divine
- A life not aligned with their values
- Poor body image, habits
- Substance abuse
- Lack of trust in inner wisdom or intuition
- Unprocessed emotions
- Harsh judgment of self and others
- Feeling alone, not asking for help
- Deep loneliness
- An inability to forgive
- No expectation of having what they really want

I looked at this list long and hard. I searched for a way to describe the women I wanted to serve and support in overcoming the repeating patterns—and to help manifest a kind and loving world. What were the common elements among the women I wished to serve?

I was called to create a new business model that went far beyond Dawn Morningstar Coaching LLC; I wanted to inspire the women I was deeply committed to serving. I explored thought-leader Seth Godin's writings on "heart-centered entrepreneurs." I adapted some of his survey questions to help identify and serve our "tribe" (his word) and define their unique needs and desires.

Describe the challenges of a representative woman in my "tribe."

She doesn't fully believe in herself, does not realize her power, and does not experience enough (if any) love, honor, and respect. She may have unfulfilling relationships, feel alone, and sometimes feels unsafe being herself. She wants to live in a better and kinder world.

Clearly describe what your tribe member already believes.

She wants something greater to experience, create, do, or be in the world—but doesn't necessarily know how to get there. She needs to be reminded and inspired in new ways. She may not feel others cheering her on. She may be subjected to those who dissuade or ridicule her. She may be tired. She may be distracted with real issues and created issues (trauma/drama) that are self-sabotaging cover-ups for lack of belief in self. She has put the needs of others first (children, spouse, job, aging parents, and so on) and has felt that it's her job to build up others, help *them* thrive and be successful. Only leftover energy, time, or resources (if any) could be hers.

Describe her fears.

She is afraid she's not good enough. She fears missing the clarity and support needed to succeed; she fears failure or that she may be disliked if she succeeds. She is afraid she is either not educated enough, too inexperienced, or too old. She may fear that her contributions and her very being are not valued by culture and society. She may believe she will never have the deepest and most sentient part of herself understood or honored. She may feel over-whelmed because her life is too complicated and stress-filled. She may feel like a fraud. She is afraid of ending up alone.

What does she think she wants?

She wants some relief and to nurture herself and maybe others in a new way.

What does she *actually* want?

She wants to love and be loved. She wants to be happy. She wants her life to make a difference. She wants to give birth to her true self, live her life fully and authentically, and be valued for what she does (finan-cially included). She wants a connection with and sup-port from others on the same path. She wants to be witnessed/seen. She wants to be heard and respected.

What stories have resonated with her in the past?

Stories of people who have wisdom, courage, honor, and value, and stories of overcoming adver-sity, and tales of people doing good in the world inspire her and touch her soul. Stories about women who live happy and fulfilled lives resonate with her, even when she feels some envy or jealously about their success.

Who does she follow, emulate, or look up to?

She is attracted to those who boldly practice living on purpose—those who practice integrity, authenticity, and courage. She emulates women who have triumphed over great or difficult challenges or hardships. She is inspired by women who reveal themselves fully and share their vulnerabilities, challenges, and mistakes—and are unapologetically human.

Mother Theresa comes to mind for her service to the poor and disenfranchised, as does someone like Meryl Streep for her astounding and long acting career and her work on behalf of women. Hildegard von Bingen, a personal heroine of mine, flashes before me for her numerous contributions to the world—all during a time when women were allowed to do very little. The list is long: Marianne Williamson, Oprah Winfrey, Louise Hay, Brené Brown, Doreen Virtue, Byron Katie, Malala Yousafzai, Maya Angelou, Caroline Myss, Karla McLaren, Esther Hicks, Christiane Northrup, Pema Chödrön, Elizabeth Gilbert, and so on.

What is her relationship with money?

Though being as financially responsible as she can be, she may support people or causes she can't really afford. She may be afraid of not having enough money in her life now or in the future as she ages. Many times, she is uncomfortable because of not being paid what she is worth. She may be afraid of becoming a "bag lady."

What is the source of her urgency?

She craves more meaningful inspiration. She is tired of waiting. She is not satisfied (and perhaps unhappy) with where she is right now—even though she may cover up those feelings to the outside world. Though she believes herself to be a good person and does good for others, she wants to know that things can be better—that she can feel personal fulfillment in her life. She is frustrated because she has been seeking greater meaning and spiritual connection for some time "doing the work" (reading books, taken retreats, perhaps trying affirmations and mantras, and more). But the sense of connection to something greater doesn't seem to stick. She may feel she is losing hope. She is ripe and ready right now to feel better about herself, her relationships, and her mark in the world.

⚜ ⚜ ⚜

Progress for women over the last hundred years has included voting rights for more women, a greater presence of women in the workforce and in higher education, and a small rise in the number of women leaders in business, politics, and religion. Though noticeable changes have occurred as a result of greater participation, many women still lag behind in advancement, authority, and pay scale.

David Gaddis Ross, assistant professor at Columbia Business School, conducted an exhaustive study in 2007 to find out why businesses with more women in leadership positions have increased profitability. He observed that women's management approach was less hierarchical and more participatory than male leadership styles, and noted that "including women on a senior management team adds to the diversity of perspectives, life experiences, and problem-solving skills, all of which can contribute to a firm's financial success."[5] However, despite these factors, men continue to be promoted more quickly and paid more than women.

What causes women's presence and success in business and leadership of all kinds to be eclipsed by men? Journalists Katty Kay and Claire Shipman set out to answer this question after they observed how many women, even the most accomplished and successful, confront feelings of inadequacy and self doubt—keeping them from achieving personal and professional fulfillment and progress.

Kay and Shipman concluded that confidence is the missing link, the gap-widening factor between men's and women's progress. The two women's curiosity led them to search for the *confidence gene*. In their books, *Womenomics* and *The Confidence Code,* Kay and Shipman interviewed women in business, sports, politics, and the military to look at commonalities and exceptions tied to confidence and success for females. They found that many women feel undeserving, feel like a fraud who "just got lucky," or that men know more or are more qualified because

---

5 "Girl Power": Female Participation in Top Management and Firm Performance by Cristian L. Dezsö and David Gaddis Ross, 2007. See https://www0.gsb.columbia.edu/mygsb/faculty/research/pubfiles/3063/girlpower.pdf).

they are louder, more assertive, and exhibit greater confidence.

Facebook COO, Sheryl Sandberg, once admitted, "There are still days I wake up feeling like a fraud, not sure I should be where I am."[6]

Women don't always trust the value of what we *do* have to offer: the efficacy of *our* experiences, perspectives, and talents. Women may doubt their own qualifications and hold back from even applying for a position because they feel they don't already know all aspects of a job. Men are less likely to let that stop them. They feel more confident that they can learn on the job, while women believe they have to know almost everything about a new job in order to even apply.

Judith Beck, an executive recruiter and CEO of Financial Executive Women, tells us, "Women are less likely to take a risk on their career. Over time they end up missing out on opportunities."

Monique Currie, an All-Star WNBA basketball player on the Washington Mystics, when interviewed by Katty Kay and Claire Shipman about men in sports observed: "All the way down to the last player on the bench, who doesn't get to play a single minute, I feel like his confidence is just as big as the superstar of the team … For women, it's not like that."

---

6 "Imposter Syndrome: Why do so many women feel like frauds?" by Claire Cohen. See http://www.telegraph.co.uk/women/work/imposter-syndrome-why-do-so-many-women-feel-like-frauds/.

Marie Forleo, founder of B School, quotes Marian Wright Edelman: "You can't be what you can't see." Marie adds, "The unfortunate truth is that mainstream media doesn't celebrate strong, successful women, and narratives about women in the media are less than 40 percent of all content... I'm a proud advocate for girls' and women's rights. They're the most underserved and under-valued resource in the world—making up over 70 percent of the world's poor and earning only 10 percent of its income, despite producing over half its food. Research shows that women and girls reinvest an average of 90 percent of their income in their families (compared to a 30–40 percent reinvestment rate for men). So making sure women continue to rise benefits us all."

The happy news: more companies and organizations are seeing the value women's perspective and talent brings to the table—resulting in higher quality management, greater productivity and increased profitability. The Ross research confirmed as much, and women's internal knowing assures us it's true.

However, increased confidence in women is not realized by merely quoting positive affirmations, telling ourselves we are worthy, and puffing up our posture. True confidence comes from deep within a woman's being through awareness, aligning with her higher self, making conscious choices, and taking action. This is the philosophy and practice of the venerable woman.

Sheryl Sandberg reminds us, "Fortune does favor the bold, and you'll never know what you're capable of if you don't try."

❧ ❧ ❧

When I first embraced the term "venerable women," I searched for images related to *venerable* online. In a Google search, men's faces dominated entire pages of photos, drawings, and portraits. Where were all of the women? Why did the majority of entries with the word *venerable* precede men's names? Where were the venerable women? I was surprised to find the domain name venerablewomen.com available and obtained it immediately.

The victors and those in power write history, and those figures have rarely been women. The stories of venerable women, even those who did important work in science, medicine, exploration, and other areas of human development, are barely mentioned in history books. We must read between the lines and do meticulous research to learn more about each woman's venerability, nobility, and courage.

I never cared much for history classes in school. With a few exceptions, the textbooks and lessons felt dry, boring, and irrelevant—who won this battle or that skirmish, how many casualties on this hill or that shoreline, the creation of certain treaties or agreements. I preferred learning about how people lived, what was important to them, and how their culture evolved. Women in history, albeit scant, tweaked my interest. The Catholic schools I attended emphasized learning about saints.

My favorite stories were based on the history of women saints like Hildegard of Bingen, who fascinated me. She was born in 1098, the youngest of ten children, and grew up in a time when most children, especially girls, were not taught to read and write, unless, like Hildegard, they were from an aristocratic family.

As a child, Hildegard began to experience "visions," later considered to have been induced by severe migraines. In light of her visions and in order to stay in good standing in the church (the tenth child from each family at that time was typically dedicated to the church and given as a tithe or offering), Hildegard's family sent her to a Benedictine monastery. This meant her life would likely be spent in complete enclosure, in a cell as an oblate (an extension of a religious order). However, her visions, and the theories and the research that arose from them, contributed to her lifelong creative work. Hildegard left the protection and shelter of the monastery and founded two convents, one on the Rhine River near Bingen and in Eibingen.

Her prolific body of writings surpassed most of her male contemporaries in medicine, theology, nature, music, cosmology, and poetry. Her writings were a source of inspiration to German Emperor Frederick Barbarossa, Catholic bishops and cardinals, and Pope Eugenius III, among others. She would have been an impressive individual in any era.

Hildegard created seventy poems and nine books. She composed liturgical compositions and religious drama. Two of her books contain medical and pharmaceutical advice, including the healing properties of various herbs. Dr. Wighard Strehlow, research chemist and author of *Hildegard of Bingen's Spiritual Remedies* (Healing Arts Press, 2002), assessed the saint's remedies and healing principles, finding many relevant and helpful in modern medicine. In 2012, Hildegard of Bingen was recognized as a saint and a Doctor of the Catholic Church, a rare title, designating that her writings and teachings were inspired by the Holy Spirit.

Hildegard seemed like a rare jewel to me and an ideal role model. I have listened to her ethereal and enchanting music for years and even as I wrote this book. Though she lived in a time of extreme limitation for women and was essentially given away by her parents, she was unencumbered by barriers and remained aligned with her highest self.

Learning more about St. Hildegard piqued my curiosity to see what other women's gifts and offerings I could uncover. Grand feats and simple acts by women have made numerous positive differences in the world.

Lyric poet Sappho was born around 620 BCE in Greece on the island of Lesbos. Sappho was both adored and maligned; her image appeared on coins and her sexual orientation toward women sparked ridicule and moral outrage. Just as Homer was called "the poet," Sappho was called "the poetess." Plato referred to her as "the tenth Muse."[7]

American grade-schoolers know about colonial hero Paul Revere and his midnight ride to warn of the British army's arrival. But another hero, not found in *my* history textbook, was Sybil Ludington, daughter of American Revolution militia volunteer, Colonel Henry Ludington. At age sixteen, she rode her horse, Star, in freezing rain at night more than forty miles (twice the distance Paul Revere rode), to go to each of the men's farms in her father's regiment and notify them to reassemble for battle. The 400 troops successfully defeated the British. Sybil Ludington was commended by General George Washington who came to her home to offer his gratitude to her.[8]

British writer Mary Shelley, born in 1797, wrote *Frankenstein; or The Modern Prometheus* at age nineteen, virtually inventing the genre of science fiction.

Famed poet Lord Byron was the father of the lessor-known Ada Lovelace (Augusta Ada Byron, Countess of Lovelace). Ada, born in London in 1815, showed a gift for mathematics as a young child. Though not customary at the time for girls to receive mathematics or science instruction, her mother insisted that Ada do so. As a teenager, she

---

7 See http://www.poetryfoundation.org/poems-and-poets/ poets/detail/sappho.

8 See https://www.nwhm.org/education-resources/biography/ biographies/sibyl-ludington/.

was mentored by inventor and mathematician, Charles Babbage. The two worked together on the earliest computer models, and Ada became an early computer programmer.

Clara Brown overcame tremendous obstacles in her life. Born a slave in Virginia in 1800, she married another slave and bore four children. Her heart was broken as family members were sold at auction and the family was split apart. Clara spent years searching for her lost family, became a businesswoman, founding a successful laundry service. She located some of her children, reunited what family was left and, along the way, helped many slaves to freedom.

Pitching for the Chattanooga Lookouts Class AA, Jackie Mitchell was one of the first female pitchers in professional baseball. The very first was Lizzie Arlington in 1898. In an exhibition game against the New York Yankees on April 2, 1931, Jackie struck out both Babe Ruth and Lou Gehrig. Just days later, Jackie was banned from both minor and major league baseball by Baseball Commissioner Kenesaw Mountain Landis because baseball was considered "too strenuous" for a woman.

Irena Sendler was a Polish nurse and social worker who defied the Nazis and is responsible for smuggling 2,500 Jewish infants and children out of Nazi ghettos in Poland. American historian Deborah Dwork described Sendler as "the inspiration and the prime mover for the whole network," noting that about 400 of the children were directly smuggled out by Sendler herself. When Sendler was caught by the Germans in 1943, she was tortured, brutally beaten, and had her feet and legs broken. Her spirit remained unbroken though, and right before her scheduled execution by the Nazis, her death was prevented by a member of Żegota (codename for the Polish Council to Aid Jews) who bribed a Gestapo guard.

Hedy Lamarr was a glamorous Austrian and American film star in the 1930s and 1940s. She partnered with composer George Antheil at the start of World War II to jam Nazi communications. Lamarr and Antheil developed a radio guidance system using spread spectrum (a form of wireless communication) and frequency-hopping technology—now incorporated into Bluetooth technology and Wi-Fi, as well as CDMA, a channel access method used by various radio frequencies. Hedy Lamarr and George Antheil were inducted into the National Inventors Hall of Fame in 2014.

At age twenty-five, Cecilia Payne-Gaposchkin, a British–American astronomer and astrophysicist, proposed an explanation for the composition of stars. Astronomers Otto Struve and Velta Zebergs described her PhD thesis, "Stellar Atmospheres: A contribution to the observational study of high temperature in the reversing layers of stars," as "undoubtedly the most brilliant" astronomy thesis ever written.

With these and many other stories of women's important contributions, how is it that women are so often diminished and overlooked?

✤ ✤ ✤

Though information about women's elevated or respected roles in the past may be refuted in some cases, there is enough evidence to suggest that women were revered and respected at various points in human history. In certain parts of the world, we can still see evidence of this.

The Mosuo people in China live near the border of Tibet. Women live in their own homes separate from their children's father (the father contributes to childrearing in his own home). Women make all business decisions and men generally make political decisions. Property and family name passes from the mother to her children.

In Indonesia, the Minangkabau embrace a matrilineal lifestyle; all property passes from mother to daughter, and the people believe the mother to be the most influential and valued members of society. When a woman marries, she is given her own place to sleep. Though she may share her bed with her husband, he is expected to leave by sunrise so he can have breakfast with his own mother. The chief of the clan is always a man, but he is selected by women and can be stripped of his leadership role at the discretion of the women. The Akan people of Ghana, the BriBri of Costa Rica, the Garo in India and Bangladesh, and the Nagovisi people in New Guinea are all women-centered in either leadership or matriliny, or in some cases both. In New Mexico, the Acoma Indians are a matrilineal society in which families take the mother's surname and the youngest daughter in each family is the inheritor of the family's dwelling.

Much has been written and surmised about previous cultures where women held more powerful roles. During the Stone Age, women may have been considered equal to men in many respects—for practical reasons. Their roles as healers (gathering and using medicinal herbs as cures, nurturing the sick), procurers and preparers of food, and those who presided over birth and death, assured their respected and necessary place in their societies' survival and perpetuity.

Lithuanian/American archaeologist Marija Gimbutas theorized the existence of a female-centered era between 7000 BCE and 3500 BCE. Based on her archaeological research into statues and artifacts of ancient Greece, Turkey, and England, Gimbutas proposed that in the time before its destruction, a "matristic" culture existed—peaceful, nurturing, goddess-honoring cultures that traced their descendants through the mother's lineage. Societies of peaceful, egalitarian farmers guided by efficacious women were later overtaken by male warring forces from Central Asia.[9]

In *The Chalice and the Blade* (1987), cultural historian Riane Eisler pointed out how matriarchy and patriarchy both result in a "ranking of one half of

---

9   *Societies, Networks, and Transitions: A Global History*, Craig A. Lockard, Houghton Mifflin, 2008.

humanity over the other." As an alternative to either term, she suggested a male/female partnership model, based on "linking" rather than "ranking," which removed the hierarchical aspects between genders—what Gimbutas referred to as the "dominator model."

Dominance by either gender threatens the potential for either to experience empowered lives. "Linking" rather than "ranking" promises greater partnership, integrity, and dignity. Power *within* and power *with* one another illuminates the venerable path for all people to live with honor, love, and respect.

Part iv

Venerable Living

The inspiration to create a way for women to expand and transform into their fullness blew into my life on a sacred breeze. I did not have any way to describe my calling in the beginning. Many women's groups were already supporting and inspiring women in meaningful ways. What could I offer that would add value in a unique way?

The word *venerable* landed squarely in front of me a short time before my kitchen plea to all women who came before and are still to come. It seemed to me that the time had come for women to trade in old ways of being islands unto themselves for a way to stand together as a continent of love, honor, and respect. There are few things as moving as the sound of women in meaningful, supportive, joy-filled and real connection, conversation, and action. I set about seeing how I could make this contribution.

V-Words

Many women have told me they were drawn to the term "venerable women" even before really knowing fully what it meant. The word made them *feel* good.

On YouTube, I searched "venerable women" for the V-Attitude video series I created and was asked, "Do you mean *vulnerable* women?" The same thing happened on Google when I first searched for images of venerable women. And no, Google, I did not mean *vulnerable* women or *venereal* women!

Consider a few more words that begin with *V*: validated, valued, vagina, velvet, verdant, victorious, vicarious, vital, visual, virgin, visited, visual, vivacious, vocal, vociferous, voracious, voyaging, vulnerable, and vulva. Many of these words actually align with what it means to be a venerable woman. The shape of the letter *v* is a triangle, the symbol of the Feminine Divine. *V* looks like a container, a cup, a chalice. The alchemical/magical symbol for water is a downward pointing triangle that symbolizes flow. This same downward pointing triangle is an ancient symbol of femininity and a representation of female genitalia. Water, one of the four alchemical elements, has the properties of being cold and moist, and symbolizes intuition, the unconscious mind, and the enclosing, generating forces of the womb. When paired with the fire triangle, symbol of the Masculine Divine, or the upward moving force, the image created is the Seal of Solomon. This symbol is commonly referred to as the Star of David. In order for the pairing of Sacred Feminine and Sacred

Masculine to occur successfully and joyfully, both must be understood, acknowledged, and honored. Each human has both masculine and feminine elements.

Prayer and inner listening on my part became key to a process to create a symbol or logo that illustrates the Venerable Women movement. I listened for the ever-present, available, and loving whisper of intuition and inner wisdom from the Divine. I went deep, asked the Collective (the word I was later given to describe the women of the Feminine Divine who guided me) for an image to capture the spirit of venerable women, and I set about letting that image find *me*.

First I did an online search for images, typing in *images* and *venerable*. Mostly I was brought to images of men and only one or two women. I wondered why more women were not shown. So I engaged a local graphic designer, a woman young in years yet old in spirit.

The final Venerable Women symbol had five dots, suggesting the heads of angels or women with their arms outstretched in blessing and connection with others. In numerology, the number 5 is the most dynamic and energetic single-digit number. Though the numeral is considered to have a mix of masculine and feminine qualities, 5 is slightly more feminine, without submissive qualities.

The symbol for Venerable Women, with its green color, associated with the heart chakra representing love, suggests spring shoots sprouting new growth. Some see the shape of a five-pointed star in the center. For me, one point represents spirit and the other four points represent earth, air, fire, and water. We thrive when all elements are acknowledged, understood, and embodied in wholeness and balance.

Venerable Attitudes

The cornerstone of the Venerable Women movement is the V-Attitudes. When a woman consciously chooses to align with her highest and best self, all kinds of magic begins to ignite in her world and in the world beyond her.

The V-Attitudes emerged and deepened my own practice of spirituality and self-discovery.

I began to feel a change coming for the V-Attitudes, but I had to go deeper on a pilgrimage for greater clarity. What happened next gave me clues for the path forward.

In September 2015, I spent a month on a personal spiritual journey in India. I spent more than two hundred hours—mostly in silence—learning from *dasas* (enlightened monks), chanting, praying, connecting deeply with my Divine, asking for my heart's desires, healing, and assessing my beliefs. I slept on a little cot in a dorm room that housed seventeen women, ate Indian food for breakfast, lunch, and dinner, and while walking to the meditation hall each day, endured high temperatures unlike anything I had ever experienced. At the end of it all, there was a greater integration of many spiritual and self-awareness concepts I had learned and practiced over the years. A deepening formed within me that went beyond words and continues to support my journey of illuminated service—to self and others.

This trip took me deeper into a healing process I thought was complete. I saw childhood abandonment and the relationship with my parents through a wider lens. As I healed and evolved, I saw how I could add my own healthy ingredients to the collective consciousness stew.

That month in India transformed my life in profound ways; I came back to the United States ready to finish writing this book—a project I had already spent nearly two years on.

When I looked at the original twenty-seven V-Attitudes, now like old friends, I felt as though I was "breathing the breath" of the woman I was then. Now I had grown. I knew what I needed to do. I had to simplify the list. Each V-Attitude would be clearer if taken down to its core essence.

I was compelled to create a sacred space in which to make a sacred request—because the V-Attitudes felt and feel holy to me. I turned on some revered music and lit candles and incense. I walked through my house and gathered up everything I could find that felt infused with the energy of the Divine Feminine—little statues, pictures, books, hearts, crystals, prayer beads, scarves, and essential oils. Then my eyes landed on a small plaque usually kept on my writing desk. The plaque shows a raised figure of a woman carrying a bowl that she lifts high as though making an offering. I love the woman on this plaque because, even as she is serving, she stands in strength—as though she has plenty to freely give. If there were water in her bowl, it surely came from a full well of her own making.

I brought all these objects into my kitchen and carefully arranged each item in the space I now held as sacred. I stood with arms outstretched to the heavens and called upon every woman who had ever lived and every woman who would ever be born, asking humbly and with great emotion, for their guidance. I was crying, begging really, as I asked, "What is it we need to *know*? What do we need to *do*? What do we need to pay *most* attention to? Who do we need to *be*, in order to live as venerable women? Please tell me, and I will be your scribe and your voice."

I waited, feeling as though I was breathing the breath of all of those women. Much more than muses, they were here with me. I could feel their presence powerfully, real in the moment. They seemed glad, glad that I asked them for their help and glad I was listening. I truly believe the women had been waiting to be asked.

I put my computer away and handwrote what I heard and felt from the women's guidance, continually asking, "Is this it? Is this how to say it? Is this what you mean?"

On the last piece of paper in front of me, I wrote a final version of the V-Attitudes.

With tears of gratitude I danced all around my kitchen. My little dog Pica (peeka), bewildered at first, started hopping around the wooden floor with me. I knew I had what I needed because it came from the collective consciousness of the Feminine Divine.

There are twelve V-Attitudes. I love the number twelve. According to Joanne Walmsley, of Sacred Scribes, "The number 12 represents the completed cycle of experience, and when an individual reincarnates as the number 12 they have completed a full cycle of experience and learned of the possibility of regeneration toward a higher-consciousness. They belong to a group of developed souls who have accumulated an unusual inner-strength through many and varied lifetimes. They may still, however, be hindered by old habits that need to be changed. The soul then attracts what it needs as a learning experience. A reversal of negative thoughts can bring about very favorable and positive effects and can aid in achieving their goals and aspirations."[10]

In each of the twelve V-Attitudes, I saw a pattern. Each V-Attitude is simple, inspiring—and easy to remember. The first four V-Attitudes we categorize as HONOR—honoring yourself, and your relationship with yourself. The second four V-Attitudes are LOVE—loving the Divine—and deepening your relationship with your Divine. The third set of four

---

10 "Numerology and the Vibration of Numbers." See http://numerology-thenumbersandtheirmeanings.blogspot.com/2011/05/number-12.html).

V-Attitudes is RESPECT and focus on a woman's active relationship with others.

The Divine is whatever deeply inspires or helps us have an experience of a Higher Power, something bigger or grander than ourselves. Some may call it Source, or God, Spirit, the Universe, Allah, Mother Mary, Jesus, angels, saints, Krishna, or Buddha. Some know nature, meditation, or writing as their transcendent inspiration. Regardless of the names we use, our intention to connect with our Divine, higher self is what matters.

Using the V-Attitudes

The V-Attitudes inspire and provide a "how to" hear the voices, essence, and guidance of the women I called upon (the Collective). They are present each time I look at the V-Attitudes and are especially potent when I practice them fully and share them with other women on the path.

Embracing and practicing the message of each V-Attitude promises a better life as part of a community of practitioners who manifest a kind and loving world starting in their own lives. They (we) heal old wounds, model positive behavior and possibilities for others, and have greater overall confidence.

Benefits of V-Attitudes include greater clarity and focus for achieving dreams and goals, restoring faith in self and others, and making deeper connections with all of life. V-Attitudes provide peace and sweetness—and an easy-to-follow roadmap back on track when feeling lost or challenged and/

or for a quick tune-up when feeling sluggish or off. V-Attitudes increase awareness of our own behaviors and their outcomes—and provide insight into others. Greater overall understanding will create a kinder, more loving world—our shared goal.

V-Attitudes are a proclamation of who we are as women, affirming the attributes, qualities, and virtues already present in us just as a sculptor envisions the breathtaking statue to be chiseled from a block of marble.

A woman who had begun using the V-Attitudes shared her thoughts about them at a Venerable Women Coffee and Conversation circle, "I don't want someone or something to tell me *what* to do—but I do like the idea of having a way to know *how* to do life in a better way. The V-Attitudes are helping me develop habits and patterns that make me happier overall."

Her statement reminded me of an earlier time in my life when patterns were helpful to me. When I was twelve, I discovered an old Singer sewing machine in the basement that had been my grandmother Rosie's sitting unused for many years. Since I really wanted to begin making my own clothes, I dusted it off, read the manual to learn how to oil the parts and how it worked. I called on a neighbor friend of Rosie's, a retired seamstress, to help me. Mrs. Paulis (everyone called her Mom Paulis) agreed to mentor me and taught me about fabric, patterns, and sizing. We spent a whole summer at it. By autumn, I was ready to begin sewing my own clothes (a welcome relief since Rosie still suggested I dress in old-fashioned clothes.)

Mom Paulis taught me the importance and necessity of using sewing patterns. I looked through huge catalogues at fabric stores to choose an article of clothing to sew, find its pattern number, and go through files inside giant drawers that held the patterns. Each pattern was tightly folded up inside an envelope with an illustration of the clothing on the front and some of the instructions and sizing options on the back. The patterns were printed on very thin paper to be laid over fabric, pinned down along the outer lines, and used as a guide to cut the cloth and sew the edges together—resulting in handmade clothing. The process fascinated me, and I began using patterns to create very simple items such as A-line skirts and sleeveless tops.

Throughout my teenage years, I did alterations for my friends' clothes and some for my grandmother. I loved sewing and began making more complicated clothes. In my senior year of high school, I designed a gown to wear to prom. Instead of using a store-bought pattern, I made my own pattern. That was the first of many patterns I made thanks to the kind support and camaraderie from Mom Paulis and my grandmother.

We can use the V-Attitudes in the same way—as a pattern to lay on top of the fabric of our lives, guiding us to create a garment of great beauty. One day we find that patterns may no longer be necessary, but the V-Attitudes remain as a reminder whenever they are needed.

❧ ❧ ❧

Maryland, where I grew up, borders the Atlantic Ocean and is home to the Chesapeake Bay. This mid-Atlantic state with all of its rivers, tributaries, and ocean and bay access, provides a haven for much wild life, sea life in particular.

The Maryland blue crab is given the scientific name *Callinectes sapidus*, which translates to "savory beautiful swimmer." As a child, I used to think the blue crab was our state mascot. I saw Marylanders wearing dancing crab graphics on tee-shirts, baseball caps, and beach bags. My favorite beach towel pictured a crab figure wearing sunglasses. Sometimes I saw fancy ladies wearing diamond crab necklaces on delicate gold chains. In our favorite small-town resort, blue crab graphics appeared posing on many shop signs along the boardwalk next to the Atlantic Ocean.

For humans, physical growth and sometimes emotional and spiritual growth are gentle processes that are mostly unnoticed while they are happening. For the Maryland blue crab though, growth and expansion are very risky. To expand into a larger shell, the crab must release its old, familiar, protective shell and, for a time, live precariously in a transparent, thin membrane. In this transition phase, the crab is exposed, susceptible to prey and injury, and extremely vulnerable. Understandably, the crab prefers solitude and seclusion during this part of its transformation. The crab's instinct guides it to endure a time of exposure and susceptibility and, in the end, it is transformed. Twenty-five to thirty-five percent larger now, her new shell thickens, hardens, and takes shape, and the crab claims her new expanded self.

In our own lives, transformation and its resulting evolution and empowerment may happen with gentle grace and ease. At other times, our transformations may take a path similar to the crab's—noticeably vulnerable and filled with fear of the unknown, a threat to what we know and believe about ourselves. No longer being what we *were,* and not yet what we *will* be, can feel uncomfortable, to say the least. Yet change requires us to let go and take a chance on what we *can* become. Vulnerability is an ultimately empowering process that allows us to be real and authentic as we evolve—sometimes while in our own version of a soft-shell stage. Just as the crab requires solitude during its process of transformation, we also benefit from going within and examining whatever next phase of growth and expansion we are called to and asking what we need to get there. When we do this, we access and use one of our greatest endowments—inner awareness.

We can begin to see that the process of becoming vulnerable, when experienced with awareness, intention, and understanding, is not to be feared or avoided—but is to be valued. Rather than halting our growth like a stoplight, vulnerability, as part of a transformation process, illuminates our path like a spotlight.

Each V-Attitude brings to mind a related story in my own life or in the life of someone I know. In these stories, vulnerability is a common theme—a thread that can show up while considering or practicing any V-Attitude. As Brené Brown tells us, "Vulnerability is the birthplace of love, belonging, joy, courage, empathy, and creativity. It is the source of hope, empathy, accountability, and authenticity. If we want greater clarity in our purpose or deeper and more meaningful spiritual lives, vulnerability is the path."[11]

Vulnerability is a fine tool for stitching together the cloak of a transformed life.

As we remember the Dalai Lama's statement about Western women saving our world, we liberate ourselves and others to rise up out of the sea of perceived limitations and experience new levels of kindness, love, and fulfillment. We emerge from the waters refreshed and renewed, feeling the utter joy of the Divine flowing through us.

May you use the V-Attitudes in ways that support you, inspire you, and cause you to remember who you are as your finest self—and how you choose to express that most beautiful, empowered, and loving self.

---

11 *Daring Greatly: How the Courage to Be Vulnerable Transforms the Way We Live, Love, Parent, and Lead*, 2015.

HONOR

RELATIONSHIP WITH SELF

EMPOWERMENT
V-ATTITUDE #1

A venerable woman empowers herself by using inner awareness and fulfilling the needs of her body, mind, spirit, and heart.

O ur relationship with ourselves is the most important of all. Being aware of and fulfilling our needs is the most generous thing we can do—for ourselves and for the world. Transforming our own lives first is the core philosophy of venerable women and opens the door to have the empowered lives we've secretly (and maybe not so secretly) dreamed of having.

Living with a keen inner awareness of our own needs may feel unfamiliar because we may be programmed to believe it is selfish to think about ourselves. If we are used to not having our needs met, we may not expect or believe that anything will change.

Inner awareness of what we personally need in each moment offers sweet gems on a day-to-day basis, not only during big transformations. We gain necessary clarity, we open to having our heart's desires become reality, and we are shown a path to having our needs met. By engaging in the process of honoring ourselves by recognizing and filling our needs, we find that our needs are often gently met. The beautiful and kind result is that our body, mind, spirit, and heart flourish. We experience a life we cherish more and more—and uncover our most empowered selves.

I considered the idea of personal needs in a new light while on my spiritual quest in India. On a scorching hot morning on a university campus in southern India, students gathered in the meditation hall where our classes were taught. We were happy to hear the hum of the air-conditioner and feel the cool air on our skin as our *dasa* (enlightened monk) entered the room. On that day we were to explore the concept of personal needs and their fulfillment. Inspired by some of what the dasa was saying, I began to think more deeply about how essential it is for each of us to recognize and fill other important needs beyond the basics of food, clothing, and shelter.

Our longing to be loved, needed, valued, heard, understood and acknowledged, to feel significant and connected are vital to a full and joyful experience of our humanity. The question we must train ourselves to ask is: *What do I need, and how can I fill that need?*

We must, in almost every moment, pay attention to what we are experiencing and, with our inner awareness as our guide, set about fulfilling what we may find missing. As we fill those missing parts, we go forth with renewed energy, inspiration, and confidence—because we *have what we need*. We feel happy. Our individual sense of fulfillment brings peace and plenty more to share.

The needs of our bodies may include eating clean and unprocessed food, moving our bodies, resting, drinking pure water, being outside in nature, dancing, enjoying massages, and asking our body what else it needs. Treating our bodies as temples is both sacred and practical. We are healthy and vital when we honor our bodies and feel the sacredness of our being.

Let us bless our bodies.

Our minds benefit from stimulating reading, meaningful conversation, learning, looking at or making art, listening to music, paying attention to our thoughts, or engaging in inspiring activities unique to our individual journeys. Analyzing and synthesizing information from our senses, the mind is a gift that serves us best when open for the heart to emerge in service to self and others.

Let us bless our minds.

The needs of our spirit beckon us to stay inspired in fresh, meaningful, and relevant pursuits. In this way, we feel the spiritual part of us flowing through all we do and all we are. Our spirit is ever present and blesses us by keeping us connected to higher, unseen forces—the lifeblood of our soul.

Let us bless our spirits.

The needs of the heart include being honored, loved, needed by others, respected, and heard. I love what poet Emily Dickenson once wrote in a letter—that "the heart wants what the heart wants." How we are called to experience our beautiful heart and have its needs met is unique to each of us. Loving ourselves, which can feel tricky at times, becomes effortless when we use inner awareness as our guide. When our hearts are fulfilled, love blesses us and expands beyond our kin and us, reaching out to a world in need of more love.

Let us bless our hearts.

Awareness and fulfillment of needs comes to us in various ways, sometimes with great fanfare in a big moment of realization. Other times we have a quiet and dear moment, an ethereal *AHA*, like a gentle breeze wafting in and through our being. Without awareness of and attendance to our needs, we stay locked up, Houdini style, in old patterns, actions, and outcomes. The result of practicing inner awareness and fulfillment of needs is having a magical key that unlocks every door leading into our peace and happiness.

To practice *constant* inner awareness is not as hard as it might sound. We are always thinking anyway, so let's simply tap into *what* we are thinking and needing. When a disturbance arises in our lives, we gain clarity using a simple three-step process: first we ask, *what exactly is the discomfort or disturbance I am feeling right now?* Be very specific here.

When we are as clear as we can be on the disturbance or discomfort, and then name it, the second step is to ask ourselves, "*What do I need exactly? What is my need in this situation?*"

Name the need, ask for the need to be met, allow it to be met, and then participate in filling the need. The key is asking and trusting that help will come our way in some form and then *recognizing, allowing, and receiving* that help with gratitude.

The idea is to develop deep self-knowledge and inner awareness so we are conscious of what *we* need first. Yes, I said it, *first*. And these next steps are the reason why.

Only after we have taken step one and become clear about our own specific need (being led to it by a disturbance or simply a conscious awareness) do we take step two: figuring out a way to meet that need.

Step three is to then ask, "What does the *other* need?" This is the three-step "Vennie" process.

Knowing, taking care of our own needs first, and then the needs of others makes a difference—and the order in which we do these is essential. We meet our own needs first, and *then* we meet the needs of others. After this three-step practice becomes part of the fabric of our being, we find that our own needs and the needs of others connect us to each other in deeper and more authentic ways.

A venerable woman in Minnesota had an experience using this three-step process, and it opened her eyes. She was meeting a friend she had not seen for quite a while and looking forward to connecting and catching up on all they had missed since they last met. The women chose to sit in the quietest part of the restaurant so they would not be disturbed while the busy lunch hour approached. Just as they were becoming immersed in their conversation, the hostess seated six women at the next table. The newcomers were hugging, laughing, and talking in loud voices—very loud voices.

The venerable woman told me she felt extremely annoyed at the six women and began to feel angry. Since she is generally a very loving person, she then felt guilty for her negative thoughts about the boisterous women.

When I shared the three-step Vennie process with her and she named her disturbance, she realized it right away—naturally she was annoyed by the noisy loud voices. The second step led her to see that her need was for meaningful connection and love. Looking back on it, she saw two possible options she could have used to get her needs met: one, she could asked to be moved to another table; or two, she could reschedule with her friend and try again. Instead she and her friend had stayed put, getting angrier by the minute without having the connection they longed for. There were no winners in this situation. From an energy perspective, the six women at the table were not feeling love directed at them, and my friend wasted a good deal of time upset about the whole situation.

We talked more about it, and she saw how being aware of her need to connect with her friend and fulfilling that need would have been a higher way for all concerned. Now that she was using inner awareness to see how she could become aware of what was disturbing her, what she needed, and how to fulfill that need, I invited her to apply the third step. "What," I asked her, "do you think the *six women* at the table needed?"

The venerable woman looked at me with a somewhat surprised look on her face as she realized the truth of the situation. She answered, "I believe *they* wanted to connect, too! They just did it much louder than my friend and me!"

In this process, the needs of the other may not turn out to be the same as our own, as they did in this venerable woman's story. Most times they will not, yet practicing this method fine-tunes our inner awareness to ultimately benefit everyone involved. There's a saying, "If Mama's not happy, then nobody's happy." So let's make sure we are happy!

We know ourselves deeply in this process and by tending to our needs—our bodies, minds, spirits, and hearts are rejuvenated in waterfalls of joy. The quenching waters of inner awareness and personal fulfillment supply not only wells in our own lives, but flow out further and further in all directions, like a dam being undone. We transform our lives into ones we truly cherish and live empowered and whole.

"We are all butterflies. Earth is our chrysalis."
—LeeAnn Taylor

Highest and Best Self
V-Attitude # 2

A venerable woman embodies her highest and best self by safeguarding her values, accepting what is, and being authentic.

Imagine a woman who had many responsibilities, duties, and commitments in her complicated life and chose to take two weeks each year to be alone. This woman went to the seashore and inhabited a tiny dwelling she decorated with shells from the beach, bits of washed up seaweed, and driftwood. When she first arrived at her little haven, she wore the heaviness of her life like a heavy shroud around her shoulders. Pale and weary, the woman found it difficult to let go and be present.

After a day or two, walking along the ocean's ever-changing edge, feet in soft sand, and eyes gazing at the vast horizon of the sea, she began to feel tranquility wash over her. Gathering shells and observing the tides with their dancing waves and glistening rainbow spray revealed her soul to her, and she felt its beauty. This made her laugh out loud with joy.

One morning when she awoke, the woman smelled the scent of the ocean as if for the very first time. Her eyes appreciated the morning light, pink and dear, and her ears captured the sound of the ocean rolling over itself reminding her of timpani in a grand symphony. The woman rose out of bed, walked upon the smooth wide-planked wooden floor, and followed the rays of sun that decorated the wall of the tiny kitchen. There she stood pondering jars holding coffee, loose tea, and dried oatmeal on the well-worn shelves.

The woman sat with her coffee and felt its heat comfort her hands through the smooth terra cotta mug. Her eyes followed the vapors of the rich brew, wildly fragrant and steaming, as they rose up out of the cup and toward the clear jars and covered tins on the old cupboard. Looking at the various canisters and feeling such peace as she did in that moment, our sea-inspired friend began to take inventory of what was important and sacred within the container of *her* life. Inspired and refreshed by the sea breeze wafting through the gauze curtains, she examined her existence anew and began to listen to its messages for her—which became clear as the ship's bell she heard ringing in the distance. The woman knew it was time to decide and put into words what she held dear.

She started off making mental notes of all the values, qualities, attributes, elements, and characteristics that were really important to her, vital really—"deal-breakers" if not present in her own life and in her relationships with others. Honesty and truth telling, kindness, humor, follow-through, consideration, healthy living, and consistency were a few words and phrases that came to her at first. The woman wanted to remember everything she thought of her during this hallowed time—and felt the importance and power of what she was doing. She began recording as much as she could in a journal she had begun writing in a few years ago and hadn't since. Our relaxed, peaceful, and inspired friend saw how good she felt when she took time to examine and align with the most highly resonating part of her being. She was glad to have explored and captured in writing what was vital to her happiness and peace—not just in this time away, but going forward in every moment of every day.

Later that morning, she strolled along the beach with the journal cradled in her arm. Sparkling and twirling waves in the ocean witnessed the vow she made to herself: she would honor and protect her values, accept what she could change (and could not change) about her life, and be authentically herself in as many ways as she could. Our venerable woman knew in her heart that this year's visit to the sea was different than others because she had gained great clarity and focus by honoring what was important to her—and a realistic plan for elevated and happier living had naturally evolved out of that process. She felt in her bones that next year when she returned—she would be joyous and peaceful right when she arrived—and her two weeks away would be a celebration of her life, not a refuge from it.

❧ ❧ ❧

Harmony, gentle joy, and a sense of empowerment are clues that tell us when we are having an elevated, joy-filled experience of life. The *highest self* is the most sacred part within each person and the *best self* is the outer expression of that sacred part in our everyday lives. Like two wings of an eagle, internal and external elements are necessary for this elevation.

Truth that resonates in our bones, inner knowing of what feels right, and virtues held in esteem are housed in sacred containers in the upper room of the *highest* self. The door to this hallowed chamber is open at all times to its architect, a venerable woman storing her treasures. When these prized possessions are accessed and offered to the world, a woman lives her *best* life.

Take a moment to visualize such a holy chamber or upper room of your own. What qualities, virtues, and attributes of yours are already there? What would you like to add? How do you bring your treasures into the light of day, and where do you hold back?

When we look at the structure of the upper room of our highest selves, we see it supported in three ways: by safeguarding our values (establishing and honoring boundaries), accepting *what is*, and being authentic.

Boundaries as safeguards can conjure up images of walls, fences, and barriers—as a way to keep out things and people. In the old paradigm (formed in the Piscean Age), a personal boundary could be seen as a castle moat, designed to keep out enemies. Even now in the Aquarian Age in which the Feminine Divine reigns and inspires love and inclusion, we may think of boundaries as a way to separate ourselves from something or someone—as a way to protect ourselves. We may still see boundaries as a line of demarcation, our *Keep Out* sign.

Boundaries do indeed, and sometimes rightfully so, serve as a way to keep *out* undesired things and people—and that is surely one way to use them. Another way to use boundaries is to identify what we cherish *within* ourselves—those values, attributes, and qualities we love (and need) and intend to safeguard. Holding what is dear and valued inside a holy container of established boundaries preserves them and because those values and virtues, attributes and characteristics, are known, and conserved—the confidence to bring them forth in our lives increases. This is a process of awareness.

Envision an egg shape of golden light around you, and see it as your sacred container to keep safe and available all you hold dear. You may think of this golden orb shape as your aura, boundary, or what is sometimes known as your proprioceptive territory. The space around you emanates out like rays of the sun of your soul into the world—and establishes the life force that is uniquely your own. If you hold your arms outstretched side to side, front and back, and above your head, you will have a sense of your energetic domain. This sacred boundary is part of you at the grocery store checkout line, as you wash your dishes, while walking down a dark street, or as you have a heart-to-heart conversation with a dear friend. Your sacred aura is always present and holds the essence of *you* and all the virtues, attributes, and qualities you value in a loving embrace. Within it is your power, your presence, and your one-of-a-kind vibrational energy field.

What do you value? What do you hold dear? What do you care deeply about? What brings you peace? What makes you *you*?

The answers to those questions will show you what to place inside your golden boundary for safe-keeping and expression.

Identifying, loving, and safeguarding the most cherished parts of ourselves is a worthy use of a boundary—and aligns us with our highest and best selves. Valued parts of the self are fortified, and secured values and attributes such as kindness, loyalty, joy, love, freedom, respect, honor, courage, and compassion are ready to be shared in our interactions with others—and with the most important interactions of all—the ones we have with ourselves.

When a venerable woman establishes a healthy boundary for herself and honors the boundaries of others, an elevated response to every situation emerges; her wisdom leads her to stop violating what she holds dear within her own boundary and within the boundaries of those she loves and cares about. Safeguarding and honoring boundaries places a healing balm on every situation because everyone feels respected for what they value.

I had a client years ago who found herself saying yes to almost everything she was asked to do. In our coaching sessions, she would talk about this a lot and how she felt exhausted by everything she was doing. She began to feel she was not really giving her best in most of the things she was doing, resulting in neglect of her own family and friendships, and herself—and found that she was *resenting the very things and people she wanted to help and support.*

She and I discussed how safeguarding her values could come in handy for practical, everyday situations in her life. When asked to do something she *really* didn't want to do (and learning to listen to her inner wisdom when it told her NO), she learned to pause, think about how what was being asked of her aligned with what was important to her, and then decided on its rightness for her from *that* deep and authentic place. *If it doesn't line up with my values, it is not going to happen* became her motto and practice. She felt empowered by her thoughtful choices.

The days of saying *yes* out of a sense of duty without contemplation, or because *it has to be done and somebody has to do it,* or out of guilt, shame, or responsibility are over. This way of being does not serve. Whatever we choose to do, be, or say does best for others *and us* when it comes from our highest and best selves—and then the energy we give out is sparkling and helpful.

Another pillar in the foundational structure of the higher self is acceptance—accepting what *is* or what *was* regarding our suffering. Accepting what is does not necessarily, and in most cases is not the same as, *agreeing* with it or even *liking* it. That's where a woman can get stuck. She may think if she accepts something painful that happened (divorce, rape, incest, torture, her own past mistakes or disappointments), she is in some way condoning it. To open the door to her inner peace (an element of being her highest and best self), she accepts and acknowledges *that the event occurred,* not that it was right or desired.

Another important aspect of acceptance is accepting oneself. One of the most effective and honoring ways to have the physical body one desires, for example, is to begin loving and accepting the body as it is right now—and go from there. Honest acceptance of shortcomings in any area of life is an important starting point. Condemning or disrespecting oneself, such as for past misdeeds or poor judgment, blocks us from fully accepting ourselves. The venerable woman is emancipated by practicing self-acceptance.

Peace and freedom are the gifts received from accepting what is. When a woman does not accept what is, she drives along the shoulder of the highway of her life with a wobbly tire. Accepting what is moves her into the passing lane with ease and grace. Her vehicle is then free to pass by that which no longer serves.

Acceptance is a great teacher—and the knowledge and understanding gained from it demonstrate the real and helpful concept that *everything happens as an instrument for inner growth and expansion.* When we awaken and adopt the belief that the Divine is "conspiring" for our evolution, we comprehend that *all* of the choices we have made and the events we have experienced are threads in the rich tapestry of our life's progress and unfolding. We live this life and past lives to evolve. Awareness of embracing a path of evolution leads us to accept what *has* transpired, without condemnation. We then use our free will and discernment to *go forward* creating and attracting *new* circumstances that better align with our values, dreams, and desires. This creates a better future for us.

Acceptance and belief in transformational evolution liberates us to forgive ourselves and others. If everything is playing a role in our evolution, is there really anything to forgive? When we think of everyone performing roles in the play of life (a life of transformation and evolution), at the end everyone gets a standing ovation. We all win.

⚜ ⚜ ⚜

Henry David Thoreau tells us: "Know your own bone; gnaw at it, bury it, unearth it, and gnaw at it still."

One of the finest ways to live an elevated life aligned with our higher self is to practice authenticity. When being authentic we embrace the truth of who we are at our core, the parts we love *and* the parts we long to improve or transform. Accepting that humans are imperfect yet excellent is a start. We see that people are a work in progress—possessing the capability to grow in the direction of the sun (higher truths and transcendence) sprouting forth from a rich bed of fertile soil (varied components of being human). Many elements must be present to create the compost in a garden—some of which might seem smelly or undesirable! The alchemy of the varied parts of compost coming together and turning into something brand new is a magical process and the same is true for personal transformation. Authenticity is valued as a way to love oneself and move in the direction of wholeness and acceptance.

Until authenticity is understood and becomes a welcome practice, an avoidance of telling the truth about ourselves to ourselves may stand in the way of receiving authenticity's benefits. This is very normal and most humans do some version of this—we may overinflate our view of ourselves by looking at another and the mistakes *they* are making, and tell ourselves we are the "good or right" ones, and by extension, they are the "bad or wrong" ones. If not paying attention, we can do this with politics or religion, people we disagree with, people who make what we judge as incorrect choices. This disingenuous approach leads people away from seeing themselves as *they* really are. Seeing themselves as they are holds much more value for them than judging themselves against the backdrop of *others*.

Another way authenticity may escape us is by telling ourselves we are not good enough. (That's a lie. We *are* good enough.) The truth of it all is in knowing ourselves and accepting the idea that we are a mixture of many traits—and we are all evolving and changing in every moment. The venerable woman lives aware of her whole self, and loves and accepts herself, flaws and all. This gives others permission to be themselves authentically as well—and then we are *each* furthering acceptance and its resulting peace together.

I love practicing *sweaty-palm truth telling*, as I call it. That is when we tell ourselves the truth, because unlike Jack Nicolson's character in the movie *A Few Good Men*, shouting, "You can't HANDLE the truth," nothing could be more off base. We *can* handle the truth. It is our salvation. Telling the truth to ourselves and to others does best when done with compassion and good timing. It feels good to be trusted with the truth—it is in the space anyway, so let's acknowledge it—and use it to set us free.

Authenticity offers another gift: the freedom to embrace and honor what we are *really* feeling. A lovely way to get to the core of the genuine self is to use inner awareness and truth telling to assess the true emotion being felt in the moment. Emotions and feelings may become masked or hidden over time and do best when they are acknowledged, felt, and expressed.

Karla McLaren, author of one of my most treasured resources, the book *The Language of*

Emotions: What Your Feelings Are Trying to Tell You. (Sounds True, 2010) invites us to recognize, acknowledge, and honor the messages in *each* of our emotions and to understand that all emotions are important, necessary, and desirable—and each one plays its unique role in the unfolding of our human experience. When emotions go unexamined, without their messages to the psyche being heard and honored, they come out sideways in one way or another. (Anger that seems to come out of nowhere, depression when one "should" be feeling happy, jealousy toward a friend's success, fear of what seems to be irrational, are a few ways unacknowledged emotions and feelings can show up.) The practice of being true to what is really being felt leads to the expression of the authentic self. Greater stability and trust and consistency come about when a woman knows her own "bone," feelings, and emotions.

An ongoing practice of authenticity creates a helpful opening for real and true feelings of discomfort, pain, grief, sadness, and fear to be safely laid upon the altar of the Divine; it is a meeting point with the Divine wherein vulnerability can lead into greater healing, understanding, and wholeness. Vulnerability is one path to transformation. The butterfly, like the Maryland blue crab, without its vulnerable (caterpillar) stage, would not emerge.

When being authentic, passion and purpose in life is ignited and the genuine self emerges in meaningful ways moment by moment.

When the essence of the V-Attitudes is practiced, there is surely a benefit for us personally, and always a benefit that extends to others. When a woman stops hiding her "shadow" parts from herself, and gets real, she gives permission for others to do the same. Then she begins to see that all humans are part of what I describe as a collective consciousness stew, each person dropping a healthier ingredient into the pot by way of thought and action.

We were not designed to be perfect, but we can be excellent. Perfection comes from the mind, and excellence comes from the heart. Excellence is doing the best we can do in the moment; and when we are being authentic, we *are* at our best.

Our human bond is deepened when we remember that it is not our perfection that makes us valuable as people; it is our authenticity and wholeness that does. In our authenticity, we meet our Divine, others, and ourselves at the highest level.

A new way of being is called for in these times, a fresh experience of women living aligned with their highest and best lives. Venerable women must not hold back any longer—and instead deliver our brightest and truest selves—in bigger and bigger ways. The time for pussyfooting around is over.

> "There came a time when the risk to remain tight in the bud was more painful than the risk it took to blossom."
>
> —Anaïs Nin

WORTH
V-ATTITUDE #3

A venerable woman affirms the depth of her worth by accessing her finest self, making inspired choices, and doing what is hers to do.

When my daughters were in grade school, there was a teacher the students adored, as did many of their parents. This teacher was a sparkling young woman, dedicated to the children and among the most creative and effective teachers I had ever known. She brought an old-time claw-foot tub into her classroom. She lined the inside with squares of colorful carpet remnants. The students went wild when they saw it and asked if they could sit in it.

She said, "Yes, but you have to earn it."

She described several ways a child could earn a "soak" in the tub: the student could do very well on a test, do something kind for another student, read a book over the weekend, or take an action that demonstrated learning improvement or good citizenship. A student who earned time in the tub could bring a book of choice and sit in the tub and read, or in some cases bring a favorite video game and play! The "soak" made the student feel special, and the other kids wanted in too.

Because I volunteered at the school, teaching art appreciation, I was in classrooms quite a bit and observed this sweet bathtub ritual firsthand. I saw how this teacher made choices that resulted in elevating her students' self-esteem. She did what was hers to do.

If a line were drawn horizontally across a piece of paper, all of the qualities and virtues that are highly resonating and desirable (love, gratitude, kindness, compassion, inclusion, honesty, and joy) go above it. Below the line are lower-resonating qualities (fear, thanklessness, ill will, animosity, exclusion, deceit, and woe). This teacher practiced what I think of as "above the line" living—practicing those behaviors that Abraham Lincoln referred to as the "better angels of our nature."

The students imitated their teacher's behavior. I noticed they became better not just in scholastics but also in human connections; they seemed to tap into *their* best selves by being kinder to other students and being more polite. Their behavior was more peaceful than children in the other classes I taught.

The teacher received excellent performance reviews overall by fellow teachers and staff, and her students did well on their test scores. However, because she was a young and enthusiastic new teacher who wanted to make lots of changes, she ruffled the feathers of some teachers who had been there for up to twenty years. When the teacher became eligible for tenure (a permanent position in the teaching field), she was denied this opportunity. She was devastated and demoralized—as were the parents and students who had experienced her unique and effective teaching. Parents wanted more teachers like her in classrooms in the field.

I felt called to try to shine light on this situation so this beloved teacher could gain tenure—and continue her magical ways with the students. I learned that if enough parents signed a petition and went to the School Board, the issue of her tenure could be examined again.

Working with a few other parents, we created and circulated a petition to obtain the required number of signatures. The teacher's tenure issue was placed on the agenda for the upcoming school board meeting. When the big day arrived, the meeting room was filled to capacity. Local cable TV cameras captured the proceedings, which added an air of excitement and anticipation for the positive outcome we desired. After hearing both sides and a short time of deliberation, the board came back with their decision. *The teacher would be tenured!* She came running up to me crying tears of joy and thanking and hugging all of the parents.

I received a call from her a few years ago, her voice filled with emotion and gratitude, and she thanked me for the role I played. She was in her twentieth year of teaching and said she loved it just as much as she did the day she and her husband dragged the heavy old tub into that classroom so many years ago. The teacher said that, had she not become tenured, she probably would have stopped teaching back then.

When we access that high place within us, make choices accordingly, and take action from that place, we reveal and affirm our own worth and increase the feeling of worth in others. This teacher did that by aligning with her higher self, choosing "above the line" ways of being, and doing what she was inspired to do. The students, by her example, did that as well—figuring out how to be their best selves, do better in their schoolwork, and behaving in ways that were respectful, kind, and helpful to others—which earned them a coveted "soak" in the tub of worthiness.

❧ ❧ ❧

Though every life has worth, women may lose sight of our worthiness. One of the reasons for this is due to the way the mind processes our personal sense of self-worth and worthiness. Our brain, our mind, ego mind, that thinking part of us, is a valuable asset that serves us well in many ways. What we may not pay enough attention to however, is that the mind requires proof—it wants supporting evidence that what we are telling it has legs, that it is "true." The mind wants confirmation of our *belief in our own sense of self-worth.*

For many years I believed I could affirm a sense of my worthiness by simply *telling* myself, "I am worthy, I am worthy." I have heard other women say they tried the same thing, reasoning that they could *think* their way to worthiness. Even when others tell us, with great fervor, that we are valuable and "worth it" (if we are lucky and blessed enough to have that happen), an authentic knowing of worthiness does not ring true because the mind has not received the evidence. What a paradox!

Though each person is inherently worthy, it is not until one links with the "above the line" self, makes conscious choices from *that* part of oneself, and then does what needs to be done, that the mind begins to accept the existence of personal worthiness.

Being abandoned as a child played a huge role in my own lack of belief in my worth and value. As a Catholic girl, sitting on a wooden pew in church and striking my chest, repeating along with the priest "Lord, I am not worthy. Lord, I am not worthy. Lord, I am not worthy," part of the Catholic Mass I attended each Sunday as a child, didn't help the cause of increasing a sense of worthiness!

Uprooting false beliefs that cause women to lack a sense of worthiness is a diligent process that happily has a positive outcome. Have you ever had a task you needed to take care of and found yourself avoiding it—to the point that the avoidance took up more energy than performing the task itself—and not doing it caused shame or guilt? We all tend to do that from time to time. When we *do* complete the task we've been avoiding or do something we *know* we would benefit from doing, how do we feel? We feel great. A series of instances, accumulating over time, when failure to access the finest self and do what needs to be done, cause a hidden consequence—a diminishment of sense of worth. The opposite is also true: when we access our higher self, make choices from that conscious place within us, and *then* take thoughtful action, we reveal our worth to ourselves and affirm it in meaningful and real ways.

We send a powerful message to our mind and to the Universe, when we say, "See, I aligned with my higher self, I consciously chose how to proceed, and did what was mine to do. Now there is movement." Taking *any* action is not sufficient. Many of us have tried doing something, *anything,* to make us feel better. But by being very clear on doing what is *ours to be and do,* and *then* taking action our sense of self-worth expands—and shame and guilt are assuaged.

America's "everyone gets a trophy" syndrome, which began a few decades ago, probably grew out of a sweet notion to amplify self-esteem and feelings of worthiness in grade school students and kids who played sports. By giving *everyone* a medal or trophy just for showing up, it was reasoned that each student would feel good about herself or himself. The problem with that notion is that it does not invite students to go within, make choices from their best selves, and then take action. It required nothing of them except to show up. Instead of increasing a genuine sense of self-worth, it seems to have instilled a sense of entitlement. The same thing can happen at any age to anyone, with less than desirable results—because the mind has not been given proof that worthiness has been earned. Inspired action is the evidence.

When practicing alignment with the higher self, and doing what needs to be done, a real benefit emerges: one stops being a victim waiting to be saved. Empowerment and self-worth increase with each action taken that is aligned with the values and virtues held in esteem.

This concept came into play the day I made one of the most profound decisions of my life: to go to the funeral home and meet my mother. I was doing what was mine to do after making a conscious and inspired choice. That choice did not come about lightly, but was a thoughtful and deliberate one, bolstered by prayer and accessing my higher self. Had I relied simply on my thinking mind, I could have found every reason in the world *not* to subject myself to what might have been a very painful and possibly unwanted reunion. Instead I went *because* of accessing my higher self first, before taking action. My mind would have wanted proof it was a good idea to go—and I could not have that proof until I went. My sense of worth was affirmed many times over the years because of using that process. My mother benefitted greatly as well. She was able to spend many years with her daughter by her side and experience her own worth and value as a loving mother. Inspired action led to an increased sense of worth for both of us.

Is there something you are called to do or be that you are avoiding?

When you access your finest self (the part of you that resonates as the "better angels of your nature"), how are you supported in making an inspired choice to take action?

What are you willing to *do*?

Once you take action, how will you acknowledge and celebrate yourself in ways that highlight your renewed and affirmed sense of self-worth?

Take a moment to go within, and answer the four questions above with as much honesty as you can. See what is revealed to you, trust what you know to be true, and commit to enter into an agreement with yourself to do what you are called to do. Notice how your sense of worth and empowerment increases in real and palpable ways as you take action on your own behalf. Do not fear your power; welcome it and know it creates your legacy.

It is never too late to begin doing what is ours to do, consciously coming from the higher self. This dynamic of living changes everything. Alignment with the higher self, inspired choosing, and thoughtful doing reveals and affirms the true depth and scope of a venerable woman's worth—to herself and to the world.

> "We don't realize that, somewhere within us all, there does exist a supreme self who is eternally at peace."
>
> —Elizabeth Gilbert, *Eat, Pray, Love*

CREATION AND
MANIFESTATION
V-ATTITUDE #4

A venerable woman creates and manifests powerfully
by using intention, intuition, and feeling.

We create our own reality. On the surface of that statement, there is so much to consider and it can raise some scary questions. For instance, does the idea that we create our own reality mean I created the circumstances that led to my mother leaving me and not coming back, as well as all the pain that followed? Does it mean that the teenager who dies suddenly in an auto accident created that experience? What about something painful or traumatic in your own life—did you create it?

If before being born, and in accordance with the Divine, we co-created an overall purpose for this lifetime, why would we choose anything but fabulous, loving, prosperous, healthy lives? Our reason for entering into a "soul agreement" before our birth is to live in a way that gives us the opportunity to fulfill our agreed-upon purpose and bring about our own personal growth. Throughout different lifetimes, we can know the depth of the human experience in many different ways and from various perspectives to develop compassion, empathy, and understanding—all as ways to evolve. One lifetime for example, we may have wanted to fully experience being loved by kindly parents. In another we may want to experience illness and loss, in yet another go from rags to riches and then back again. We made a choice to enter this world for unique reasons involving variations of the following: expansion and learning; experiencing sense perception, feelings, and emotions; or sharing wisdom and love with one another. The desire to create is a part of our constant evolution.

As those who manifest powerfully and create our reality in this life, we can think of ourselves as creators or *co-creators* who feel the support, wisdom, and guidance from our Divine along the way. None of us creates anything alone. We benefit wildly by remembering our unique power as co-creators with our Divine and with others.

Inspired by the Divine gifts of free will and the power to manifest and create, we set about learning, expanding, and evolving through varied experiences. Not all attempts to evolve are elegant or easy, to say the least. Some are downright clunky, hard, and painful. I have always found it helpful to remember that every experience I co-create, and the resulting outcomes, is truly designed for my evolution and expansion. Knowing that, I am secure in the knowledge that the Universe, our Divine, Source, God, whatever name we choose, is "conspiring" for my (our) evolution.

The routes we take on this life journey are rich, varied, and purposeful. Each person enters into her or his own soul agreement for life on this earth over many lifetimes. Every person's chosen path is worthy of respect. The most honoring thing we can do for others is to bestow compassionate blessing upon one another. In doing so, we support each person's evolution. We cannot pretend to know or guide what another has chosen to experience—or see it as wrong or less than. Remembering this, our great gift to another is to nod in deep blessing and gratitude as we pass each other along the way, walking with compassion, generosity of spirit and action, and becoming the very best version of our evolving selves that *we* can be.

I reawakened to the idea of honoring each person's unique evolution in a big way while visiting India in 2012. Many people I met appeared impoverished, yet, whether I found them in the temples I visited or on littered side streets in New Delhi, mostly every person I encountered was gracious and friendly. I could have easily judged their situations and experiences of life (and what they had manifested or created) as dire and somehow less than. Yet, they projected a sense of peace and meaning that I had rarely come across on the streets of my own shiny town in America.

I have been inspired over the years by certain Bible passages, especially ones in which I find a deeper meaning. "So God created [humankind] in [God's] own image," *Genesis 1:27* (NIV)

That we are made in the image and likeness of God is an invitation to humanity to express ourselves fully knowing that we are an extension of the Divine. I feel aligned with the idea that humans are *of* God or like God, since the essence of the Divine courses through us in mystical and profound ways.

We may sense an inner knowing that, being extensions of the Divine here on Earth, we are endowed with and gifted by elements of Source, Spirit, the Universe. Among these gifts are love, creativity, expansiveness, joy, and possibility. How blessed we are and how empowered we become when we remember that! Remembering and activating our own co-creative powers of manifestation allows us to participate in designing our life experience in new and beneficial ways.

Scientists are studying and concluding the profound effect human consciousness and intention has on the physical world. Dr. Masaru Emoto, a researcher and author of *Hidden Messages from Water* (Hado Kyoiku-Sha, 2008) took his love of water and examined how the effects of intention on water influence its molecular structure—illustrating the power of thought, feeling, and intention. His experiments led him to slowly freeze water samples from rivers, tap water, and lakes and look at their crystallization under a microscope. Water taken from city tap water, rivers, and lakes near large cities did not have the same beautiful qualities when photographed as the water from pure and clean sources that were unpolluted and natural. The clean water provided a blank slate on which he began conducting more experiments; he and his team showed various photos to the water, played music to the water, prayed over the water—and photographed the results. The more beautiful and loving the intention of the prayers, photos, and music—the greater the grace, elegance, and symmetry was evident in the photos. Loving intention bestowed upon the water made it better.

Nikola Tesla, renowned futurist, electrical and mechanical engineer, physicist, and inventor, is quoted all over the Internet as saying, "The day science begins to study non-physical phenomena, it will make more progress in one decade than in all the previous centuries of its existence. To understand the true nature of the universe, one must think in terms of energy, frequency, and vibration." The science community has taken his statement to heart, conducting experiments that prove the role energy plays in existence.

Though it is helpful to have scientific verification, many women inherently know the power that intention and feeling have in creating and manifesting. A woman simply knows certain things, using her keen sense of intuition—and she ascends to new heights as she trusts this more in her life. She sees she is much more powerful than she may have allowed herself to believe in the past. It is imperative to see, know, and practice creating and manifesting in new ways. Reawakening to and embracing the ability we have to create and manifest is a welcome gift the venerable woman opens for the world—and shares.

The old saying, "The road to hell is paved with good intentions," rang out when I first used the word *intention* in this V-Attitude. I really want to negate that old feeling, perhaps change it to, "The road to *heaven* on earth is paved with our intention, intuition, and feeling." Like many old sayings, the idea simply needed updating to match our new awareness.

Think of intention as focus. When we focus on what we long to experience in our lives, use our intuition to guide us and our feelings to manifest, we receive concrete results. Intuition is the ability to understand something almost immediately, bypassing conscious reasoning and thinking. For some it's a knowing, for others a feeling in the body or a focus in the heart. Some hear a "still, small, voice." However intuition shows up in our lives, it is best when cultivated, trusted, and acted upon. Many find intuition to be much more trustworthy for guidance than thinking alone. How does intuition support us to co-create our life experience and evolve? Simply, it is a direct connection to the wisdom of the Universe, our Divine, transcending our own little slice-of-the-pie wisdom, which is baked with our personal limited view and experience of life. Using intuition is like having the wisdom and love from the entire universe as our personal Divine pie baker, at our disposal at all times. Yes, let's have that pie, please.

Esther and Jerry Hicks, who share the teachings of Abraham in their book, *Ask and It Is Given: Learning to Manifest Your Desires* (Hay House 2004), invite us to think of this human experience as one in which feeling and emotion are among life's greatest gifts. They go as far as to suggest that feeling feelings, the senses, and emotions, are primary reasons humans want to have this experience of life on earth—and that feelings are powerful building blocks to construct lovely lives. The ultimate gift and desire that fulfills us most, is to arrive at and live in joy.

We become what we *feel and what we embody.* We manifest through the power of our feelings, coming from the heart and becoming real in the world. If we long to have a loving relationship in our lives, we daydream and imagine and *feel* what it will feel like to have that in our lives. We feel it and feel it and feel it, and then feel it again. We feel it in our bodies; we see it as though it is already happening. This process works to attract heart's desires of all kinds—a new home, a new car, a gift for someone we love, more money. We delight in *feeling the feeling* of having what we want—and then *see it manifest* in our lives as our life experience. Feeling what we long to have or experience or be with as much zeal as we can muster, as though it has already happened attracts it to us. That is a Universal law.

Through feeling deeply, we come from a place of passion. Passion is the excitement under the feeling—like the wind in the sail of a boat. Having deep feeling and passion sets us toward the shoreline of what we would like to see made manifest. Floating around in the waters of all things we can choose, we do best to pick a spot on the shoreline using our intention. With our feelings and passion, we set our course in *that* direction.

Mata Amritanandamayi Devi, known as "Amma, the hugging saint," has used the feeling power of love to heal, bless, and uplift over 33,000,000 people. She evokes powerful feelings in the many people of all ages, races, and religions that she holds in her arms, and creates in them a sense of peace, joy, or whatever they may need. Amma travels around the world and hugs thousands of people each day, for many hours a day, offering feelings of love and acceptance to all who wait patiently in line for her. *New York Times* journalist Jake Halpern interviewed Amma in 2013 and asked her how she was able to maintain her energy while hugging so many people. She answered, "I am connected to the eternal energy source, so I am not like a battery that gets used up."

The ability to create and manifest powerfully comes from the eternal energy source Amma referred to. In this Aquarian Age in which the water element reigns, fluidity and Spirit are the forces that allow manifestation to occur in the physical. Matter can be affected with intentions set forth as seen in

Dr. Emoto's experiments and certainly in feeling, as witnessed in Amma's simple hugs.

This V-Attitude demonstrates the eloquent connection between our feelings and what we manifest—for ourselves and for others. Each of us can break free from the burden of painful past experiences through self-knowledge and self-love, opening ourselves to live our personal lives with joy, abundance, and creativity, and ultimately transcending to providing meaningful service beyond ourselves.

What does your heart desire? Take time to name it, using all of your senses and feeling, and feel it as though it is already happening. Hold your intention like a focused laser and use your intuition to discover how it can unfold for you with grace and ease. This is your right; this is your power—your gift to and for yourself—and for others.

Using intention, intuition, and feelings as the perfect magnets to attract what we long to experience in our lives reminds me of Wooly Willy Magic Magnets. The first one I saw and played with as a child in the 1960s was a thick piece of cardboard with a man's face imprinted on it. Over the man's face, which had no hair or eyebrows, was a clear plastic cover filled with tiny metal filings. Holding the face flat, I used the magnetic wand to attract and arrange the black pieces of metal to create hair on the man's head, eyebrows on his forehead, mustaches, and beards. It felt like magic to me to arrange, attract, and create as many iterations of the man's face as I could dream up. When we think of our intentions, intuition and feelings, as the magic wand of our Wooly Willy Magic Magnet life, there is no end to all we can attract, create, and experience in our own lives. Our magic is Universal law in action.

Manifesting powerfully is within our reach, waiting patiently for us to lean forward, go within, and focus our intention, use our intuition, and feel our feelings. In this way, we are created in the image and likeness of the Divine.

The venerable woman uses the powerful creative juices of feeling to manifest in her life. She raises up her intention, intuition, and passion like lifting a newborn to the sky, examining its beauty and possibility, holding each to her chest with love and gratitude.

> "It is not your job to make something happen—Universal Forces are in place for all of that. Your work is to simply determine [and feel] what you want."
> —Esther Hicks, *Ask and It Is Given: Learning to Manifest Your Desires*

LOVE

RELATIONSHIP WITH
THE DIVINE

TRANSCENDENCE
V-ATTITUDE #5

A venerable woman delights in a transcendent relationship with her Divine by committing to meaningful spiritual practice, receiving fresh inspiration, and living in sacred union.

During my month-long personal spiritual journey in India in 2015, I received teachings and training from enlightened monks, both male and female, called *dasas*. Before meeting the dasas, I was told of their high states of consciousness and envisioned them to be Zenlike, quiet, tame, and uninteresting. I wondered what I had gotten myself into. After the first five minutes with our morning instructor, a woman dasa with a shaved head and sparkling brown eyes, I saw how my assessment of the dasas could not have been further from the truth.

Because the dasas spent a great deal of time in their own personal spiritual practice, they were serene, present in the moment, humorous, and self-assured. They were the most loving people I'd ever

met, not superficial in any way, deeply prescient—
and wise beyond words. The dasas taught truths
about the human condition that showed each of
the sixty students from all over the world that we
were understood and honored. We laughed at our
human foibles and saw how humanity is much more
interconnected than separate.

As expected, the dasas were present and calm,
thoughtful and brilliant; however they were fully
engaged in modern life. They used technology effi-
ciently—air-conditioning cooled the meditation
hall, electric lighting and music boomed through
huge speakers to set the mood, laptops controlled
presentations on large screens, and microphones in
various languages could be relayed to participants
by translators.

We began our days at 7:30 in the morning and
completed our training about twelve hours later.
This was our routine seven days a week for twenty-
one days. Students learned to chant in Sanskrit (an
ancient Indian language), did ecstatic dancing (moving in ways that allowed the Divine to flow through
the body), practiced meditations that took us deep
into our souls, and examined our beliefs and values.
The dasas led us in rituals to heal from past hurts,
becoming more whole than most of us had ever felt.

During that extraordinary experience it became
apparent to me that daily spiritual practice infused
with meaning and substance are key to having an
elevated experience of life, peaceful and closer to
the Divine. Greater clarity and real ways to love were

some of the gifts we would gain in the days to come. Because many of us vowed to be in silence for the twenty-one days, we were able to have a rich inner life free of distractions that can sometimes come from discussion and processing thoughts and revelations with others. Though it was hard for me not to talk (*really* hard sometimes!), and a few times I did talk, overall I stayed true to my vow of silence and received meaningful benefits because of it.

During the second week of our instruction, I felt a profound shift in my own spiritual practice. Rather than daily meditation and commitment to spiritual principles being something to strive for, something to *do*, they became a feast provided freely to nurture my life—sustenance that nourished my soul and gave me energy and vitality to be the woman I came to this earth to be. This loving commitment to stay in transcendent relationship with my Divine delighted me. Remaining in sacred union became simple and sweet. I wondered how I would be able to continue this easy and grace-filled connection with my Divine when I returned to the "real" world.

One morning, I arose with the sun, showered in the communal dormitory bathroom, and quietly dressed in white linen clothes (which we were encouraged to wear because of the heat and to honor the purity of our intentions for spiritual growth). Many of us had begun wearing bindis (a dot or small jewel worn near the third eye) to signify spiritual awakening. I gave it a try and used false eyelash glue (recommended by an American woman who had worn a bindi for many years). My bindi was a beautiful tiny effervescent round jewel and after a few attempts to get it centered, I looked in the mirror and, though a bit shy about it, felt a sense of the sacred. I left it on. I gathered up items and placed them in my backpack: my journal and favorite pen, bottled water, photos of loved ones, and a list of nearly two hundred requests I had collected from family, friends, and clients fulfilling my promise to hold them in prayer while in India. Walking along the grounds of the University with the intent to sit outside before the heat of the Indian sun made it sometimes uncomfortable to do, I searched for a place to connect with my Divine, pray, and process some of what I was learning.

Scanning the lawns, which were meticulously manicured by Indian women and men workers, I spotted a dasa who appeared to be deep in prayerful meditation. She was dressed in orange flowing robes, sitting on the grass in what appeared to be a sacred posture. I admired the dasa's commitment and felt inspired to be more like her. Trying not to disturb her meditation, I carefully walked by her to sit by a beautiful tree I had seen on the long walks between my dormitory and the meditation hall where our daily classes were held. When I looked down at the dasa, I saw that she was leaned over her laptop with earphones on—Skyping with someone! She smiled up at me and continued her conversation, laughing and talking. In that moment, I saw how the sacred and the ordinary are one—and to see them as separate prevents us from a consistent and holy experience of life overall. The visual of the monk on her computer remains with me and inspires me to see all of life as a sacred adventure, here on this blue planet spinning through the universe and blessed by the Divine.

Many women on the spiritual and self-awareness path embark on journeys to enhance their connection with the Divine. Reading inspirational books, attending sacred gatherings or retreats, listening to CDs or live-streams, frequenting presentations by inspired thought leaders—and traveling across the globe for holy pilgrimages are all ways to receive fresh insight and meaning. Walking in nature, lighting a candle, and breathing in the fragrance of incense or essential oils creates an atmosphere and an opening to oneness with the Divine. Taking in the beauty of sacred art and chanting or dancing can elevate the soul and soothe the mind. There are numerous fine ways to connect with the Divine, and the search for fresh inspiration is a lifelong and worthwhile one.

Some women are led to a spiritual practice through the religion of their childhood, and others discover and craft their own unique path of spiritual expression and experience. A combination of elements can evolve and comingle over time to create meaning for the spiritual seeker. When in pain, one may pursue and find comfort and answers from connection with a higher power, something greater and wiser than ourselves. Individual devotional and holy paths help us see with new eyes, feel with healed hearts, and experience blessing in everyday life.

Every time we commit to practice union with our Divine, we are making a living, breathing statement: *I am telling my mind that I want my heart to be in charge.* When we purposely choose to connect with our Divine, we infuse our lives with greater clarity and guidance for making decisions both big and small. We find ourselves being more understanding and compassionate toward others and ourselves, we attract abundance with less effort, and we find our relationships organically healthier. This is a commitment worth making and keeping.

When discussing commitment to a meaningful spiritual practice, a woman said to me, "Commitment is such a serious word. It feels heavy. I don't like it."

Anything that gives great benefit is worth commitment. Brushing our teeth is one example, as are preparing healthy meals, taking a walk in the fresh air, and sleeping enough. Relationships require and benefit from commitment, as does creating "white space" (free time) in our days. We must take responsibility for what is important in our lives—especially when we know the impact it has on our own happiness and joy factor, and consequently for the entire world.

The door to the Divine is always open, waiting for anyone who chooses to step through it. Consistent meaningful spiritual practice, when fresh and relevant, makes it easier to listen deeply to the voice within. Some call that voice the Soul or God, others call it the Divine or Source, and still others call it Super Consciousness, the Higher Self, or Nature. There are hundreds of names we can give the Divine, and hundreds of names people have used over the centuries to connect with the God of their understanding. How blessed we are to have this voice available to us at all times. I am delighted when I can share an experience of accessing and listening to that inner voice with a friend or client—and certainly when I practice it myself.

Many times as part of an opening ritual in coaching sessions or group gatherings, I create a sacred space to breathe into the moment, be still, and listen. I love watching women relax, become peaceful, and come into the present moment feeling the presence of their Divine. It is a palpable transformation to witness.

Committing to a regular and defined practice is a game changer. I'm not certain the Divine needs this—though I am convinced *each of us* does. We need spiritual practice and ritual to bring us to the place of oneness with our Divine—not as a mental concept—rather as a true and real-time experience of the living Divine for which our soul longs. We are called to plug into the Universal Source of All—from within our hearts. Staying engaged with the Divine is key.

It is not important *what* we do for our spiritual practice, it's *that* we do it. The practice we choose needs to resonate with us, nurture us, and connect us to our Divine—and may change over time.

Spiritual practice and ritual is like physical exercise; it needs to be something we *like* to do—or we won't do it. Certain kinds of physical exercise would probably be much more effective for me than what I do now. Yet, when I have tried them over the years, I did them for a short while and stopped not only that exercise, but also all other exercise. That's how it can be with spiritual practice and ritual. We are called to explore what resonates with us and *stay* with that. We are building our spiritual muscles and inner transcendent health when we do.

Becoming present, using the breath, and quieting the mind are ways to tap into sacred union with the Divine. The mind wants to keep up the chatter—and seems to amp it up even *more* when we try to quiet it down. It's as if the mind knows we are trying to be still and decides to introduce old and new ideas with rapid force! That is because the mind alone cannot feel and does not understand our need to connect with our Divine. The mind, being based in logic and outcomes, functions by keeping us chock full of thoughts, which makes it challenging to settle down enough to feel our heart and what lies within. Our hearts are ready and waiting for the real deal.

Here is my version of a practice I learned in India to quiet the mind. I call it Flowing Like Feathers. You may increase the time to do this, making sure to keep each of the three steps approximately the same amount of time.

1. Allow for the river rush of thoughts constantly already in your mind to be there. Don't try to do anything with them at all. Don't censor them or try to make them stop. Let the thoughts do whatever they want to do. Do this for two minutes in the beginning. I set my mobile phone alarm for this. Breathe into this.

2. Now allow for any and all thoughts to enter the mind, but this time, place each thought into a category sending it down a cascading waterfall. For example, if you have a thought about an upcoming bill to be paid, put it into a category you name Money and send it down the waterfall. If a thought comes in about what you are going to buy at the grocery store, you may want to create a category called Food and place the thought in that cascading waterfall. There is no need to overthink the category; allow it to come naturally and it will. Do this for two minutes. Breathe into this.

3. When thoughts come into your mind now, place them in single file, one after the other. One by one, allow the thoughts to go flowing by like feathers on a lazy river. Feel the peace of this. Do this for two minutes. Breathe into this.

Practicing and creating sacred ritual on our own in solitude is beautiful, as is being in the presence of others for spiritual gathering. Practicing alone and in groups benefits those on the path. The gatherings can be in person or online—or even by phone.

There are a plethora of choices for spiritual connection. We can find a spiritual tribe that aligns with us by exploring what's out there. We become magnets of grace gravitating toward one another so we can pray, learn, become more inspired, meditate, sit in stillness, and breathe together. It is merely a matter of asking and committing. Now is a great time to be alive; there is so much to support our spiritual journeying!

Spiritual seekers are discovering and exploring new approaches and elevated outcomes in regard to their practices. Women appear to be attuned to this after many years and varied practices that involve writing affirmations on Post-It notes, creating vision boards, and quoting spiritual passages.

Ideas, concepts, and principles learned about spirituality, self-awareness, and consciousness are like a bucket on a rope (the mind) being lowered and lifted into the deep waters of the Divine (the heart and soul). Now is the time to *stay* in the refreshing, replenishing, healing well waters and ultimately *let go of the bucket all together*. Remaining immersed in the sacred waters of the well of love, thirsty lives are rejuvenated, calmed, and renewed. Oneness with the Divine is no longer a mental concept, a wish, or an occasional high. Instead of *thinking* and learning more and more about how to be kind, compassionate, and loving, those who choose to commit to a meaningful spiritual practice receive fresh inspiration for the path, and listen deeply to the voice within, delighting in a personal and tangible experience of the Divine on Earth.

This new way of being in relationship with the Divine works best when moving from thinking and hoping spiritual principles are effective, to *embodying* the essence of these universal and holy principles. Women are ready for this extraordinary time of awakening. Many men are awakening as well.

There has been an inner knowing that something much more was beginning to emerge, something seen in the glowing embers of the soul. Seeking, finding, and staying committed to meaningful spiritual practice fans the flame and increases light from the fire of inspiration. This inner knowing is similar to that felt by "lightworkers"—individuals who have volunteered for a sacred charge, chosen before birth, to provide healing in their own lives and in the lives of others on earth. They are healers and teachers performing kind acts.

Everyone is playing her or his role in Divine evolution. Venerable women carry the fire of transcendence in their hearts.

> "You create a path of your own by looking within yourself and listening to your soul, cultivating your own ways of experiencing the sacred and then practicing it. Practicing until you make it a song that sings you."
>
> —Sue Monk Kidd, *The Dance of the Dissident Daughter*

GRACE
V-ATTITUDE #6

A venerable woman calls forth grace in each moment by being present, embracing peace, and engaging fully in life.

The word *grace* can conjure feelings and images of kindness, compassion, elegance, ease, and dignity. Grace is one of many gifts from the Divine to be cherished; it becomes more meaningful when fully experienced and shared. Feeling the grace in each moment is a beautiful way to live because it blesses and affirms the value of our human journey.

A venerable woman honors the presence of grace each time she comes fully into the now, keenly aware of what is occurring, standing lovingly and fearlessly in the moment. Women are the bearers of presence and demonstrate it standing at the bedside of a sick child, consoling a friend, and celebrating an important milestone in someone's life. A woman brings grace into the world during her encounters with others in many ways—with the server in a restaurant as she offers understanding when her food arrives late to the table (or cold when it is supposed to be hot) or by being present to an employee who has a personal crisis. Grace waits in each moment to be uncovered; venerable women are excellent excavators and practitioners.

The presence of the Divine is found right in the moment. One of the most effective and real ways to experience grace is to sit inside the fullness of the holiness of each moment. We feel its peace and gentle power.

When a woman brings her full attention into the present moment, she discovers and affirms *the present as the source of her power.* Presence is the sacred container for the incubation of a woman's empowerment—her efficacy expands and her heart opens to possibilities. A steadfast eternal love from her Divine flows through her, felt as guidance and a promise of her life fulfilled. Being in the moment takes a woman out of the coldness of perceived limitations and fear and wraps her in a warm blanket of peace, calm, and possibility.

Practicing being in the present moment is not always aligned with the Western culture. But it is not impossible to practice being present in a fast-paced, purposely distracting, never-have-enough way of life. Finding peace in the present increases when awareness of its benefits is realized and a way to practice spending time in each moment is found. Being present can be simple, yet it may not always be easy. Like many worthwhile desired outcomes, practice is the key. Guidance found in the sacred present can lead to a more fulfilling life.

In his book *The Power of Now: A Guide to Spiritual Enlightenment,* (Namaste Publishing, 2004) Eckhart Tolle tells us, "The power for creating a better future is contained in the present moment: You create a good future by creating a good present."

There is no other moment than this one. Over and over, a new moment emerges, fresh and new, waiting to be visited and valued. Each of these moments is the power to create the forthcoming life we desire.

Many times we hear, "Just be in the present," "Be mindful," "Stay in the moment." What does the mind do when we attempt to stay present? It gets busy!

Using only the mind to be present causes a competition among all the thoughts prattling around in the head, each one vying for attention. Monkey mind, as Buddhists call the never-ending rush of thoughts, can cause us to miss out on all that is right in front of us. The Flowing Like Feathers exercise in V-Attitude #5 is a great way to practice becoming present.

Dr. Langer, professor of psychology at Harvard University, invites us to notice, witness change, be curious, and see things we think we know inside and out—all with fresh eyes. For example, think of going on a trip to someplace new, or even someplace you've been before but not for a while, and how you will feel when you get out of the car or off the plane. The tendency in this more awakened state is to look all around discovering every little this and that, purposefully looking for all the eye and mind can take in—in a state of discovery, wonder, and possibility. This state of grace can make our everyday lives a revelation.

One experiment I tried began with filling my dog's water bowl in the morning. I emptied the bowl of the water in the bottom, watching the water pour out and down, while listening to the sound it made in the sink. I looked at the empty bowl and noticed how it appeared when it was empty as compared to being partially full. I rinsed out the bowl and felt tiny droplets of water splash against my skin.

Looking down at my dog Pica, I saw the excitement in her eyes because she knew that filling the water bowl was step one to the important next step—filling her food bowl. I felt excited with her, and for her, and found myself giggling a little. Using my senses in this simple act of filling the water bowl for my dog—noticing, engaging, paying attention, and seeing it as though it was the most important and meaningful thing in the world—set the tone for the rest of my day.

But you may ask, "Who has *time* for all that? Really, I can barely get the things done I need to do now! I am a busy person and cannot take the time to be thinking in such detail and paying attention to every little thing."

We are constantly thinking thoughts in our heads anyway, naming things as good or bad, repeating self-sabotaging statements, jumping to the future and hanging out in the past, worrying about money, body weight, diets, kids, grandkids, the Middle East, the latest disease, the weather, and on and on. If not careful, we will never *be* where we really are—and will truly benefit and be enriched when we *are*. So instead, why *not* choose thoughts that bring us into the glory of the moment at hand? This is where we unwrap the gift that is the human experience.

Peace lies within each moment. Once we remember to get in the now, into the present, we find peace waiting patiently for us to land in its arms. The simplest way to make our way to the open arms of peace is to breathe into the moment. Breathe. Into. This. Moment.

Life is a grace-filled affair awaiting our RSVP.

What does it mean to engage fully in life? It starts with saying yes—agreeing to do things and have experiences that enrich our lives and expand our horizons. Shonda Rhimes, mother of three and creator and producer of some of American television's most popular shows, explored the idea of engagement in her own life. Though an obviously busy woman with many personal and professional commitments, she realized during a conversation with her sister at Thanksgiving dinner one year that she was holding back and not fully living. When she looked a little more at the reasons she said no to invitations and experiences, she discovered it was *not* because she was too busy; it was because she was *afraid*. Shonda saw how she feared saying the wrong thing at a gathering or appearing foolish on one of the many television interviews she was invited to participate in. She decided to take one full year and say yes to everything that frightened her.

Shonda Rhimes' world opened in unexpected and welcome ways during the twelve months she agreed to engage in her life more fully. She overcame many fears, enriched her life, and increased her sense of worthiness. She shared her discoveries in a memoir called, *Year of Yes: How To Dance it Out, Stand in the Sun and Be Your Own Person* (Simon & Schuster, 2015). What would your year of yes include? How about a week of yes—or even a day?

Engaging the senses, noticing, and staying curious and open results in a sense of playfulness and helps a woman reveal grace to herself and others during the moments of her endeavors. What feels so good to us is coming from an in-the-now, inquisitive, noticing place, which leads to embodying (experiencing, integrating, feeling in the body—in a grounded and centered way) life as a full participant. We are then able to have the experience we came here to have as humans, rather than living in times from the past and unreachable times in the future. Being present and engaged improves and deepens our relationships and we tend to become better listeners!

We benefit from experiencing what is right in front of us. The eyes of a young baby looking intently at each face and searching all around in wonder demonstrate the kind of inquisitiveness that can bring adults much joy by imitating it. Perhaps that is one of the reasons we love babies so much (aside from how cute they are!). Babies live in wonder, curiosity, and amazement. What might the moments of our days be like if we looked at each thing as if it were brand new and we were seeing it for the first time? The truth is, everything *is* new. All things are changing at all times. The empty dog bowl gets filled and then is empty again. The laundry never comes out of the dryer the same way as the times before, and the taste of an apple will land differently on our tongue today than it did last week. There is much to be experienced, much that can enrich us if we peer into it with wonder. What are we waiting for?

When we are rigid in our thoughts about an experience, we can never fully appreciate its wonder. Staying open to the moment supports us to remember our most human of gifts—our senses—and helps us to be present and mindful. Other gifts are opportunities for more appreciation and gratitude in our lives. And of course we remember the high vibrational energy that appreciation and gratitude brings.

When a venerable woman is truly present, as mindful as she can be, all things are possible. Within each blessed moment we can become good friends with peace and better acquainted with our higher selves. Being in the present moment is where we commune with the Divine and express as our own unique version of the Divine in the world. The Divine awaits our coming into the present moment, allowing the chalice of our being to be filled with Divine essence and grace.

When it's over, I want to say: all my life
I was a bride married to amazement.
I was the bridegroom, taking the world into my
arms.
When it is over, I don't want to wonder
if I have made of my life something particular,
and real.
I don't want to find myself sighing and frightened,
or full of argument.
I don't want to end up simply having visited this
world.

—Mary Oliver

EXPRESSION OF THE DIVINE V-ATTITUDE #7

A venerable woman lives as an expression of the Divine by acknowledging the presence of the Divine within her, knowing her soul, and using her gifts.

A rose does not need to be reminded of its beauty. It unfolds itself from a tight bud, expands its velvety petals in the sun, shares its sweet aroma, and never veers from its nature. Perhaps that is why so many people love this queen of flora. The fragrance of a rose showing up for no obvious reason is an indication of the presence of angels as described by many who have experienced miracles or encounters with angels.

Though we may not always remember the essence of God-ness within us, the Divine always does. How might we see ourselves in the true light of our nature more if we remembered, without doubt, that our very being and actions are a way to have God show up in the world in real and palpable ways?

What happens when we become clearer vessels for the expression of the Divine? How would it make us feel to bring forth the Divine and positively impact the resonant energy of the world around us?

I recall being brought to tears when I first heard the story of Malala Yousafzai, the Pakistani girl who began receiving death threats from the Taliban because of her courageous stance promoting education for girls in Pakistan. The Taliban followed through with their plan to try to stop her advocating for girls' education by shooting her in the head on her way home from school at age fourteen. Thankfully, after receiving outstanding medical care and enduring many surgeries after a medically induced coma, she recovered. I see Malala as one who expressed (and continues to express) the Divine part of her by bringing more light to the world by furthering education for girls. As we have seen, and as we know in our being, when girls and women are educated, they and those around them lead better lives. I remain inspired by Malala's actions and how she embodies the gifts she has been given—the inspiration to serve and enlighten girls, and the fortitude and tenacity to carry on in spite of challenges and obstacles.

As we have explored in this book, and have an inner knowing from our own experiences, there are many reasons women have been conditioned to miss seeing their illumination, not trust it, or hide it under the proverbial basket. When hidden away from a world that needs more light, more love, and more of the Divine, a beautiful opportunity is missed. Venerable women remove the baskets covering our own light and help one another when others' baskets may feel stuck.

Our soul, the immortal and spiritual aspect of our being, is the connection to the Divine, like a ray of the sun. How beautiful to think of ourselves filled with the light of the Divine, there inside us at all times, illuminating our way.

I worked with life coaching clients over the years who became caught up in a tangle when they tried to think of themselves as an expression of the Divine. They did not see that each person could choose to excavate down into their soul, listen to its message, and discover the gifts that lie within. Perhaps they did not trust the messages they found at first—or trust that their gifts had value. Once they were able to trust their gifts and offer them, they began to feel freedom that blessed them.

Some questions to ask to dig down deeper and find meaningful clues:

1. What have you ever done where time seemed to disappear and you became lost in the joy or total engagement in it?
2. What have others told you about a positive quality or way of being you have?
3. When you dive deep into the well of your soul and acknowledge your gift(s), what emerges?
4. How does acting from the soul support you in expressing the Divine in the world?

5. What meaning do your actions take on when they grow out of a sense of Divine expression?

6. What, if anything, holds you back from trusting the messages of your soul and fully expressing your gifts?

8. Looking back over your life, what will you have given yourself by living powerfully and purpose-fully as an expression of the Divine?

9. As you go forward, what are you giving the world by knowing your gifts and sharing them?

"If you bring forth what is within you, what you bring forth will save you. If you do not bring forth what is within you, what you do not bring forth will destroy you," are the words spoken by Jesus. (*Gospel of Thomas,* found in Nag Hammadi, Egypt in 1945)

If we take a look around and inside ourselves, we can see that the lives we dream of living are tied directly to the gifts inside us. When those gifts (or as they are called in the Temple of Venerable Women, gift purposes) are expressed, they save us, liberate us, and deliver us to our highest good. If we do not bring those gifts forward, we experience a void that cannot be filled. God knows, many of us have tried filling that void in a number of different ways. If we don't do what we love, we may end up doing things that don't love us!

The happiest people I have ever known, person-ally and professionally, are those who figure out what it is they love—what jazzes them, makes them feel juicy and alive—and then they do it. Some have figured out ways to do what they love as their career, others do what they love in their personal, non-working lives. For many, it's a combination of both. Uncovering and bringing forth our unique gifts, talents, and deep interests, in real ways on a consistent basis, is like having a sustained lifelong orgasm—as the creative force of the Divine flows through us and brings great joy. This is expression of the Divine.

A woman's journey benefits when, from time to time, she takes stock of her gifts and how she is using them. For example, a love of partying and staying out late with friends at a younger age in a woman's life may morph into sacred gatherings or women's retreats. A love of reading and receiving inspiration might grow into a woman's own writing, sharing *her* ideas with others. The woman who loved playing dress-up in her mother's clothes may choose to express her talents as fashion designer. A compassionate child may grow into a powerful healer.

An interest in something, the interest that will not go away, must be paid attention to. It must be recognized as a message from within that longs to see the light of day. No more baskets hiding our light, remember?

Sometimes a woman's gift to the world is the fulfillment of a promise she made with her Divine before she was born—something *she* wanted to share or experience. Like a wise parent or friend, the Divine blesses us. The Divine always supports a woman's evolution; free will liberates her to uniquely do what is hers to do and be.

The path to uncovering a woman's gifts, talents, and deep interests may come about as a result of her early challenges or hurts or discomforts from the past. Transforming old pain into joy is a way to live happy and fulfilled and heals us at the highest level.

Giving our gifts and talents their due honors our Divine and equally honors us.

Living as an expression of the Divine does not mean, however, that we are perfect angels on earth. Part of our problem is thinking we have to be perfect. Perfection does not really exist for humans, and is an unhelpful and limiting construct of the mind.

Perfectionism disguises itself as thoroughness, dedication, and proof of worth. A woman trying to be perfect creates a self-imposed barrier to her greatness and can assuage this limitation by being more gentle, approving, and kind to herself. How to do this? We access the Divine in us that loves us just as we are, become clear on what we long to offer, and then put it out there. I remember a time when I would not allow the Venerable Women website to go live because it was just "not ready." Once I remembered that allowing perfectionist tendencies could prevent a beautiful message from reaching women who would benefit, I pushed the "launch site" button. We can always augment our efforts with better ideas or new information at another time. Let us move ahead expressing the gifts we have. Think of excellence as doing the best we can do in the moment; it is enough.

A beautiful freeing effect occurs when we let go of expecting perfection from ourselves and others—and embrace excellence instead. It even *feels* different in the body when we choose excellence over perfection. We feel freer, lighter, and more *okay*. Being our excellent selves is a form of authentic humility and a key to open the doors to new possibilities.

Another piece to living as an expression of the Divine is allowing the human shadow side to be seen and acknowledged. This makes us fully human and clears a path for light to shine through and bless us. As we remember from V-Attitude #2, women align with their highest and best selves when being fully authentic—and in our genuineness, we meet the Divine.

The dawning of this new time is the sunrise we have been waiting for, and women are wiping the sleep from their eyes and rising up from their slumber of self-doubt and hesitation. All of the conditions are set for this awakening. Entry into the Feminine Divine energy of this Age of Aquarius, the choice women are making to do their own individual transformations, and the desire and commitment for comity, all tell us this is so. Let us keep heart.

> "I am an expression of the divine, just like a peach is, just like a fish is. I have a right to be this way…I can't apologize for that, nor can I change it, nor do I want to."
>
> —Alice Walker

Joyful Abundance
V-Attitude #8

A venerable woman experiences joyful abundance by being grateful and generous, and believing in her innate prosperity.

Abundance is having what we need, when we need it, with some left over to share. What a simple and sweet way to think of prosperity! We can tend to complicate the idea of prosperity or abundance, or have it muddied up for us by outside factors. For years, there was a debate in spiritual circles about the difference between prosperity and abundance, with both sides extolling the "right" way to think of each one. Which word we use is not as important as understanding that having what one desires blesses and fulfills our lives—and brings joy. Venerable women value joy!

I added the word *joyful* before the word *abundance* in this V-Attitude because I have seen so many people have abundance who don't seem very joyful. We all do well when we have what we desire in the area of relationships, experiences, and material things; on this earth many things do require the currency called money. Babies cost money to feed and clothe, housing requires money, and so do transportation, clothing, and pretty things we want to have. But really, how much money does a person *need*? I read about the *Panama Papers*, an expose of many wealthy people placing billions of dollars in offshore accounts to evade paying taxes and to hide their money. I thought, *Really?* How many billions can one person or one family *require*? What need is trying to be filled by having obscene amounts of money and possessions? Venerable women are wise to this and remember we do quite well having what we desire when we want it, with plenty left over to share.

Though the American economy is generally strong, there are other economic inequities across the board—based on race, sexual orientation or identity, or age. Women in the United States still only make seventy-nine cents on the dollar compared to a man's salary—for performing the same jobs. Many families have two-person incomes and still cannot make ends meet. One in twenty American children do not have enough to eat—in the richest country in the world.

Much of the world's population lives on under a few dollars a day, and many do not have enough food to eat, water to drink, or adequate shelter. There is enough food to feed every single person on the planet every day, if it were distributed to those in need. There is enough money to house everyone and prevent or heal diseases. So why isn't that happening?

Riane Eisler, author of *The Chalice and the Blade* provides insight: "In sum, the struggle for our future is ... the struggle between those who cling to patterns of domination and those working for a more equitable partnership world." Venerable women surely fall into the category of those working for more equitable partnerships in the world—and we know in our souls that the Divine is the source of all.

False and inequitable economics are designed to keep some people feeling powerless and others feeling powerful. *It is time for this to stop.* Venerable women are positioned ideally to inspire change in this arena. How do they do that? The venerable woman transforms *the* world by transforming *her own life*. Yes, it really does work that way.

The venerable woman lives in gratitude, which is among the highest vibrations on the planet, akin to the energetic vibration of love. As she walks in gratitude for all she is, all she has, all that is around her waiting to be discovered, and all she can share with others, she ignites a fire and magnetism for more to come into existence. This is not more just for the sake of having more; it is the more that satisfies the desires of her soul in thoughtful ways and supports her in having a full life. Having a blessed and fulfilling life of our own creates fountains to share and enjoy together.

Gratitude is a multiplier, because the way to create more of anything is to align with the vibrational energy of that which is longed for. When grateful, a woman is aligned with the energetic and unlimited physical storehouse of joyful abundance. Her pursuits become effortless, yet oh so appreciated.

Generosity is the queen of hearts! When each of us has what we want, when we want it, with some left over to share, that's when the real magic happens. Plain and simple, it just feels good to share what we have. In a study done with chimpanzees in 2014, oxytocin (a feel-good hormone) increased when the chimps shared food with one another. What the observers of this experiment found most interesting is that their sharing increased bonding among the chimps—even with those *outside the chimpanzee's immediate group.*

Venerable women love to bond, to connect, and to share, and their oxytocin levels rise too, when they do.[12]

Both gratitude and generosity support us in experiencing joyful abundance. Now let's take a look at what role the woman's own belief in her innate prosperity plays. With our awareness of and trust in our own intrinsic abundance, venerable women know that there is more than enough for everyone, and that everything is possible to have, to do, or to be. This way of thinking also invites a

12 See http://rspb.royalsocietypublishing.org/content/281/ 1778/20133096.

woman to know at a core level that she is a powerful creator and one who manifests through her feelings. We remember this from V-Attitude #4: A venerable woman creates and manifests powerfully by using intention, intuition, and feeling.

We dive deeper into the concept of abundance because it is a tricky subject for many to master; not having what we want or need prevents us from living our fullest and best lives. Our Divine is the source of all and delights in sharing with us. We were born into a world of plentiful beauty and bounty, and are here to experience it fully. We may temporarily forget this, but the Divine does not.

We remember that people are having their own unique experiences for their individual evolution—and may include knowing what it is like to live in lack or poverty. If that is the case, we bless their journey. If it is not, we can choose differently. We are never victims. We are creators.

Some on the spiritual path, those who live to heal or serve others, and many who don't believe wealth, prosperity, or abundance is possible for them, may struggle in the area of prosperity. Their struggle may grow out of the idea that to serve or be spiritual means they should separate themselves from money—even if they are not consciously aware of that within themselves. Or they may believe that having a prosperous life is for *others*, not for them. I have seen this belief system show up many times over the years. But know that there is a path out of the experience of lack. There is plenty for everyone, all the time. Why *not* each one of us?

A powerful tool we can use is to take a look back in past lives for vows of poverty we may have taken at some point. This process does not have to be complicated at all. Simply go into a quiet state, be in the conscious presence of your Divine, and ask to be gently shown a time in the past when you may have said yes to remain impoverished by making a vow of poverty. This could have been as a nun, a monk, a priest, or other religious or holy servant in a past life—or anyone at all. Saying yes to that kind of vow was usually based on a person's desire to be close to their Divine, and being taught some version of, "Again I tell you, it is easier for a camel to go through the eye of a needle than for someone who is rich to enter the kingdom of God." Matthew 19:24. (NIV) No wonder this "lack" consciousness has become so engrained in the human psyche.

There is absolutely nothing wrong with choosing to live simply and with few possessions, as long as it is for a reason that makes sense to you and aligns with the life you want to be living now.

If you decide to do this looking-back process for yourself, here is a simple and effective way to do it: Once you have an idea of a time when you may have taken a vow of poverty in your past, simply go back to yourself in that life. You may not be the same sex or have the same religion or spiritual belief system you do now, but that does not matter. Be open to what you see in your mind's eye and go into as much or little detail as you like. Your goal is to visit yourself as you were then, with understanding and compassion. Bring your wise, loving, enlightened present self. Let that you know that what he or she did by taking a vow of poverty was from the heart and for an important reason, and that you understand. Then invite yourself in that past life to understand that you are choosing a new vow now—a vow of abundance, prosperity, and generosity. And let the previous you know that you appreciate the sacrifices made, but that this is a new day for you and you are ready to move on. This generous process may liberate that *you* from your past life too!

❧ ❧ ❧

I love beauty. Beautiful relationships, experiences, and surroundings are important to me. I like to live in a lovely home and eat high-quality organic food. Traveling to beautiful places around the world delights me too. All of these things and experiences cost money. In addition, my heart is happy to give gifts to those I love, and some people I hardly know—and to support causes in which I believe. It is fun for me to have a mixed experience, buying some things at full price and other times shopping for and finding bargains. I have been one who loved "fancy" things throughout my life even though I came from humble beginnings and was told, for example, "those kinds of [big, beautiful] houses are for rich people, not for people like us." This was usually said with a scowl by one of my relatives. Somehow I never believed it and inwardly knew I would live in a big beautiful house someday, which I did for several years. Then prosperity looked different to me, and I chose to live in a *small* beautiful house! Each of us has powerful attraction forces within us; they originate in a belief in and trust of our innate prosperity and abundance.

A beautiful way to attract what we want is to bless those who already have what we desire. We can feel jealousy or envy when we see someone has achieved a goal we have not yet experienced, buys a new car like the one we want, or has a grandchild when we really, really want a grandchild. Feeling the yuck of this is actually great if we use discernment to move us forward. When we are authentic and see how we may begrudge another of having something we really want, we gain clarity and focus for our own goals and dreams, get inspiration to uncover what we may need to do to attract these things, and activate the manifestation of what we would like to do, have, or be. Blessing those who possess what we want aligns us with the possibility of having it, rather than separating us as "have nots." Venerable women are the "haves" because we bless the possessors.

Another important piece, probably the most important of all, is that when asking for our heart's desires, we do not have to know *how* it will happen. We simply need to know *what* we want, and *feel* it with all our being and senses, as though it is already happening. Doing so aligns us with the energy and frequency of our heart's requests and attracts them to us. We have our steps to take for sure, yet our desires and their fulfillment are coming from our Divine, which is the source of all.

In this Age of Aquarius, it is *essential* for each of us to have our needs and desires met. Then we can freely experience the beauty of this life, serve where we are called to serve, and share all that we wish to share with open and generous hearts—without worry of lack.

I was at a talk by Marianne Williamson, thought leader, teacher, and author of *A Return to Love: Reflections on the Principles from a Course in Miracles* (Harper Collins, 1992) in California a few years ago when the topic of money, lack, and prosperity came up.

Someone in the audience asked Ms. Williamson, "How do you know when you have enough money?" I loved her response. "You will know you have enough money when you don't need to think about money anymore."

What a lofty goal for each of us! And happily, it is doable.

> "Isn't it marvelous to discover that you're the one you've been waiting for? That you are your own freedom?"
>
> —Byron Katie, *Loving What Is: Four Questions That Can Change Your Life*

RESPECT

RELATIONSHIP WITH
OTHERS

UPLIFTED LIVES
V-ATTITUDE #9

A venerable woman uplifts each life she touches by practicing compassion, unconditional love, and kindheartedness.

I once traveled to Mexico to escape Minnesota's brutally cold weather and to get some writing done. At the center of town on Isla Mujeres (Island of Women) was a church near my hotel called Inglesida de Concepcion Immaculada. All around this tiny town I saw altars, statues, and images of the Blessed Mother Mary along side streets, in restaurants, on top of cliffs, in homes, on tee shirts, and in markets. Atop the red-tiled roof of the church stood a statue, one of many iterations of the Blessed Mother that appears everywhere as a tribute to the mother of Jesus, an archetype of the Feminine Divine.

This statue of the Blessed Mother with images of the moon on dark-blue robes rises high into the Caribbean sky above the church's main door. Fresh seaweed is often found at the feet of the

maritime-themed statue of Mary in the morning—
as though she went into the sea during the night to
protect, nurture, and bless the waters. Isla Mujeres
is a fishing town and its people rely on the sea to
provide them with food and fish to sell to earn
their livelihoods. The fishers are happy to have the
Blessed Mother's consecration.

After a few days on the island, I decided to walk
into this Catholic Church. My choice was intentional
after having decided many years before to stop
attending church. I consider myself a woman who
embraces many religions and spiritual traditions.

I felt great peace as I sat on a wooden pew inside
the simple white-walled sanctuary. As I looked
around, I spotted intricately engraved gold sliding
doors in a far corner. Because the church was mostly
unadorned, it seemed odd to see such extravagance.

The surroundings evoked feelings I had as a child
when the Catholic rituals, stained-glass windows,
and smell of incense mystified me. I knelt down and
prayed the way I did back then—speaking simple,
sweet prayers, filled with love, hope, and joy. I felt the
presence of the Divine Feminine, along with angels
and saints, just as I had in childhood. My happy feelings remembered from younger days, when religion
was a source of comfort for me, were overtaken by
feelings that came about later in my life: pain, fear,
confusion, depression, anger, disappointment, and
shame. The whirling of emotions began to feel like
an unusual alchemy, and I was not sure what would
result from it all. I focused on the Divine.

As a child I was taught that God was to be feared, was outside of me, and needed to be mollified. I did not know for certain then that the Divine was inside me, as me, as an expression of the sacred in the world. I now felt comforted by the thought of having *that* God in my heart and in my life as I sat in the quiet church. I felt great joy to remember that the same God was inside my sisters and brothers on Earth, no matter what name that God was called or how God was understood or worshipped. How very beautiful it all felt sitting in that simple and sweet church.

Lost in this reverie of feelings, awareness, and understanding, tears streamed down my face. There was some sadness, some joy, some grieving, and much gratitude. No sound came, but rather the crying that comes from emotions felt and honored, like quiet prayers floating on the river of the soul.

Moments later, the golden glass door of the mysterious room opened silently—those very same closed doors which had intrigued me earlier. A small Mayan woman came through the door and seemed to head my way. She walked toward me and began speaking to me softly in Spanish. Not understanding her words but intuiting her meaning from her kind eyes and gestures, I knew I was to follow her and enter the room behind the golden glass doors.

She took my hand, opened the doors, and led me silently inside the secret room. She turned and left, closing the doors behind her without a sound. Inside were a few short wooden pews, flickering candles, and large dreamlike murals of the Blessed Mother Mary's compassionate face and graceful hands painted skillfully on the walls.

Looking back on it all now, I realize the kind Mayan woman must have felt compassion for an American tourist sitting in a church with tears streaming down her face. She gathered me up, invited me in, and showed me great kindness. My Mayan angel lady did not allow any language barrier or my confused look to stop her from sharing her compassion and unconditional love with me. I will never forget her lined, sweet face, her kind heart, and how she uplifted my spirit that day.

Just like the Mayan woman I encountered, every one of us has the power to elevate each life we touch. Sometimes it is done in a big way, like those who are full-time long-term caregivers. Other times uplifting another happens in a small way, like smiling genuinely at a passerby on the street—or waving a hand of thanks when a driver on the highway lets us merge in front of her car. Compassion is one of the dearest ways to uplift others because it offers our sisters and brothers benevolence, empathy, and kindness—the very virtues we are blessed by receiving ourselves. It costs us *nothing* to be this way in the world, and makes *all* the difference. Compassion toward oneself and others is a choice, moment by moment—and a sacred practice.

Another practice that uplifts the lives of others is kindheartedness (tolerance, generosity, non-judgment, friendliness, and goodwill). It is amazing how much judging humans do—of themselves, of others, of places, things, and situations. Some even judge themselves for judging! If not consciously aware of all this judging, we may find we live life in a courtroom of sorts, with an overworked jury (constant thoughts, monkey mind), misunderstanding facts (limited or incorrect information), and rendering many guilty verdicts (judgments). It's all very exhausting and divisive, and does not provide us supporting evidence of the love and connection our hearts desire. We know we are here to transform our world starting with ourselves. A way to proclaim innocence for everyone and to continue to uplift each life that is encountered is to let go of harshly judging others, and ourselves, and instead choose discernment.

judge: make decisions based on evidence
discern: catch sight of; recognize and understand

As we look at definitions of the words *discern* and *judge* we see a noteworthy difference in their underlying meanings. Something in the deep, kind, and generous part of us knows to choose discernment rather than judgment. Judgment requires decisions be made based on evidence—yet how can we be certain that the evidence we have is accurate and true? Each of us processes situations using limited information through filters of past experience. Judging in personal relationships is a part of the old hierarchical system; there must be a judge, some evidence, and someone to be judged. Judgment always results in right versus wrong, innocent versus guilty, good versus bad. Judging one another and ourselves ends in some form of separation—the *last* thing we need in our world. The meaning of the word *discern* is deeper, kinder, and wider than the word *judge*—and allows for greater compassion, understanding and connection.

If you were to have a conversation with someone using judgment (that kind that leads to a form of condemnation), it may go something like this:

You: "Michelle, you were supposed to be home at 11:30 to meet me for lunch. I expected to see you then. Why weren't you here when you said you would be?" (Even if you don't say it exactly like this, if the underlying intent is one of judgment that another is wrong, it still conveys the same message.) All communication, whether thought or spoken, is infused with the energy of its intent. Asking a question starting with the word *why* can imply judgment and that the other has done something wrong or undesired. I avoid using *why* at the beginning of a question, especially if I am annoyed at the other person!

Michelle: "Um, I thought it was at noon. I'm sorry." (Michelle is now made wrong and it does not feel good. She has a need to apologize and knows she is being judged. Her wall of defense goes up and she feels a need to protect herself. The separation between the two of you has begun.)

You realize after the conversation that *you* had written down the wrong time on your calendar. Using the judgment model, you used incorrect evidence as your basis and judged another to be in the wrong in the process.

The same conversation using discernment might go something like this:

You: "Michelle, I thought we were meeting at 11:30. Is that what you thought too?"
Michelle: "I had us down for noon. Well, I am glad we are together now!"

Can you sense the difference between these two conversations? You can see the way you or another person feels when being judged—using evidence that may or may not be accurate. By contrast, feel the way non-judgment and discernment allows for generous connection with one another. The basis of the word *discern* is understanding and recognition. How beautiful is that? Wouldn't we rather be understood and recognized than to be judged? No one likes to be judged; choosing non-judgment instead uplifts everyone involved.

Non-judgment and discernment employ curiosity while judgment uses certainty. The gifts in curiosity are openness, fresh perspective, greater possibility, playfulness, and connection. Certainty creates dead ends, old paradigms based on the past, little possibility for change or growth, heaviness and disconnection.

Look at our political system and religious expression in the United States—as well as other parts of the world. Certainty and judgment divide us in ways that allow for very little grace and connection. Imagine what the discourse could be if instead of judging one another, we began to understand and accept one another. Allow yourself to feel, really feel, what the world will be like when we come from a heart of understanding. It is in our imagining this and feeling it with all of our senses—as well as practicing it ourselves—that we create and experience the world we want to see.

Sometimes we judge because we are trying to impose our own point of view or desired outcome on others. We also judge so that we can have superior footing over another. Venerable women are wise and know that it is best for all concerned when *everyone* is lifted up and respected.

A woman I coached years ago divorced her husband and found she lost several friends and in-law friendships because they judged her without having all of the facts. Of course, one hears about divorce situations where people feel they have to pick sides. Yet what would have happened if the people who left the woman's life had sought to be kindhearted toward her instead of judging her? There are also times when we judge something as "good" or "bad" initially—only to discover later that what we thought was good was not, or what we thought was bad was not.

Signs of judging:

1. Feeling disconnected from yourself or others
2. Causing yourself or others to feel small and misunderstood
3. Pushing people away from you
4. Lack of trust
5. Not truly seeing the goodness in yourself or others

Being judgmental separates, non-judgment unites.

Doesn't it fill you with hope to know that these small shifts in our consciousness and behavior can make such a huge difference in our own lives and in the lives of others? Venerable women are uncovering, remembering and practicing the love, compassion, and kindness that comes naturally to them—and find that this is the key to saving ourselves and our world. Aren't you happy you are already wired this way? Sometimes we just need to dust off the beautiful circuitry inside.

This is a meaningful and playful way to increase awareness of being judgmental:

Using your beautiful intuition and inner wisdom, begin to notice the ways you judge yourself or others. Envision a harsh and angry judge banging a gavel loudly when you realize you are judging. Now create a visual from your heart to represent non-judgment, discernment, and benevolence. Your visual could be an angel, a kind being, a soft kitten—you get the idea. When you choose to discern instead of judging, bring your visual to mind. You, and others will feel and notice the difference.

❧ ❧ ❧

One of the needs for all of humanity is to be loved, and that is understandable. A venerable woman uplifts the lives of others by offering unconditional love, which some say is nearly impossible for humans to do. But it is possible to love unconditionally once we are aware of what it really means. Love without conditions is something that is generally not learned and consequently not practiced. It is *how* we love that keeps us from giving and receiving the love we truly desire.

Love with conditions goes something like this: I want to be loved, and I want to be loved in a particular way. If my beloved (partner, spouse, child, friend) does things the way I want them done (conditional), I will feel secure and *then* I will extend love. If my beloved does not follow my conditions or expectations, I will feel unloved and may withhold love from her or him.

For many, a condition for love is "I want you to love me *more* than others, and I want you to prove it again and again." Sometimes if our beloved shares love with another, there may be a feeling of discomfort or suffering (jealousy).

What many of us have learned about love is not love at all—it's more possession and ownership. For example, when we tell someone we love him or her, don't we expect to hear that in return? And don't we expect it to be said in a particular way (condition)? And don't we want actions from another to prove it over and over again?

Unconditional love that uplifts the lives of others—and raises us up along with it—is the remembrance of one simple idea: love *is*. Love is not something to be earned or deserved, it is something to be experienced, shared, and cherished.

Each day in my classes in India we were given the opportunity to share a story, a feeling, something we had learned. A woman named Francesca from Rome who was a fellow student shared a beautiful example of the existence of love, without conditions and expectations.

She shared with our group how she had originally planned to stay for just the first two weeks of the courses. After the meaningful experience she had during those first weeks, she had made the decision to stay on for the third week of classes.

When Francesca went back to her dorm room and shared the news that she was staying another week, everyone cheered and hugged her, saying how elated they were that she was staying. They danced and sang, talked late into the night—and the evening turned into a party. These women had not known one another before this experience—and like most of us, had been mainly in silence, so communication was limited.

At one point in the evening, Francesca had a moment of clarity. She discovered at a very deep level that love is not something one deserves or earns. She realized that love simply *is* and is its own sweet, dear, connecting gift, available at all times, for all people—and she felt it in a real way from the women in her dorm.

Love is not about conditions, it is not about what someone does or doesn't do. Love is always there—a choice any of us can make in any moment. It is in love that we find our own peace, our connection to humanity, our joy. It doesn't need a reason.

Who could you love in a new way, letting go of conditions, requirements, and expectations? What would be gained? How would you uplift another by loving unconditionally? I know that the dear Mayan woman who invited me into an inner chamber to my soul that day in Mexico understood compassion, unconditional love, and kindheartedness at a deep level—and so did the women in Francesca's dorm room in India. Your venerable woman heart expands when you love.

> "People are like stained-glass windows. They sparkle and shine when the sun is out, but when the darkness sets in their true beauty is revealed only if there is light from within."
> —Elisabeth Kübler-Ross

LOVE
V-ATTITUDE #10

A venerable woman loves and is beloved by inspiring deep connection, trust, and collaboration with others.

When a woman chooses to connect deeply and collaborate with others, while inspiring trust, love is a natural result. Almost anything be accomplished, created, and healed in an atmosphere of loving connection. When people come together for a common cause, honoring each voice in the group, a woman is often at the heart of it. She is embracing and advancing the idea that love simply is.

Connecting at a deep level while listening and truly hearing one another, telling truth with compassion, and collaborating paves the way for greater love in the world. As a venerable woman remains committed to this vital role competition, dominance, dishonesty, and greed fall away and are replaced with collaboration, partnership, truthfulness, and generosity. This is how love and empowerment reigns in the hearts of all people, connecting us to one another.

What does it mean to be deeply connected? We connect most deeply when we allow walls of separation to come down by being authentic ourselves and creating a safe space for others to be authentic as well. Our own authenticity gives our brothers and sisters permission to be their whole selves as well. In V-Attitude #2, we describe how authenticity allows each person to reveal the highest and best self—and how deeply we can connect when each of us is coming from that higher place within. Being authentic opens the door for an organic experience of truth telling and honesty.

Many years ago, my friend and mentor, Jeanette Monterio, and I were leaders in a spiritual center that was divided about what direction we would take moving forward. In one of many meetings about the future of the center, some people seemed to hold back about what they really wanted to see happen. Their passive energy did not feel honest. Something was off; we all felt it.

Guiding us in prayer and inviting each of us to *go within*, Jeanette created a sacred space in the meeting. She said in a very loving way, "The truth is here in the space. Let's let the truth be heard."

Some people in the meeting took her up on her invitation to tell their truth and began sharing what they *really* felt about the situation. The energy in the room immediately felt lighter because of those who spoke their truth, and we all felt a deeper connection with one another. Truth telling can often be a messy affair requiring courage and a willingness to have sweaty palms from time to time. Yet I have come to believe that messiness is part of the creative process that, when those involved behave intentionally with love, leads to something greater. Truth telling is the foundation for trust—and trust is a home for love.

Paulo Freire described love as, "an act of courage, not of fear."

Some hesitate to speak the truth because they don't want to hurt anyone else's feelings. But holding back what we really believe does not honor the other person, and will often inevitably come out sideways anyway—through thoughts held inside and felt by the other, or by gossiping or triangulating (talking to someone else rather than the person who would benefit most from hearing the truth). Telling the truth as we understand it, spoken from the heart with the intention to understand and be understood, is a sign of deep respect.

Any discussion about connection and collaboration, which leads to an experience of authentic love for one another, serves to examine what we believe about power. Old models emphasized power *over* another rather than power *within* oneself. A sense of competition led the way, in which there were leaders and followers, winners and losers, those with the ideas and those whose ideas were not considered. Rather than a circle—round, solid, stable, and inclusive—the result was more like a wobbly tower likely to fall because all voices, talents, and skills were *not* included.

Intentional commitment to practice inclusion, truth telling, and the trust that grows as a result, along with shared power leads away from a tower of competition and into a sacred circle of collaboration. Every voice is heard, and harmonious agreements are made; everyone shares the goal or mission. This is power.

We know in our bones that we do best when we work together for common good, rather than remaining separate and competing with one another. This way of being infuses our connections with love and joins us with one another's hearts. Venerable women know love and are beloved.

> The person standing on the mountaintop did not get there by falling.
> You have to climb to where you want to go—
> and you cannot get there by climbing over others.
> It is about climbing *with* others, side by side, and
> even pulling some others up with you.
>
> Are you willing to do that? If you are, you'll get to that high place, and others will be happy that you're there—which is what will keep you there.
>
> —Neale Donald Walsh

CIRCLE OF LIFE
V-ATTITUDE #11

A venerable woman embraces the circle of life by honoring her ancestors and sharing virtue, wisdom, and traditions across generations.

The circle of life is "nature's way of taking and giving back life to earth. It symbolizes the universe being sacred and divine. It represents the infinite nature of energy; meaning if something dies it gives new life to another."[13] However, the circle is not complete without including our own ancestry and progeny. Without our ancestors—we would not be here at all!

Embracing the circle of life begins by honoring those who came before us and those who are yet to come. We do not have to know all of their names, what year they were born and died, what they did, or even where they came from. Some ancestors we have

---

13 Collins Dictionary.

known, and perhaps loved deeply, while they were alive; others we may not have even liked.

A venerable woman benefits from remembering that each of our ancestors, just like each of us, was a product of all that occurred in their lives and made them who they were. Most important to know is that each did the best they knew to do when they were alive. We may be tempted to judge them and question how an action one took could have been "the best" they knew to do; yet this is true. We can see it more clearly when we look at things we have done in our own lives that were not up to par.

The gift that the venerable woman has is *awareness* of how each of us can remain locked into old patterns of behavior and mistakes until choosing to do better and breaking the chain. We are called to break free of the bonds of bad behaviors ancestors may have had, being understanding and forgiving, and replace old ways and actions with loving, enlightened ones.

Ancestors no longer here on Earth are unable to change the choices they made or actions they took when they were alive. They need us to do that on their behalf. The benefits and blessings of having "right relationships" with my ancestors was proven to me when I studied in India. The dasas taught us that until we show appreciation, compassion, and kindness toward our ancestors, we will suffer. I thought the dasas were full of beans when they first proposed this idea. They didn't know how messed up much of my lineage had been! How could any of my ancestors help me now? I was actually still angry and hurt by actions of some of them. I wanted to have them out of my mind.

Calling forth and honoring ancestors is a beautiful practice that can be life changing. Showing understanding and compassion, while granting our forebears forgiveness, frees them to their highest good in the afterlife and opens the door for them to bless and guide us in this life. Life improves in magical ways when we honor our ancestors. Finances improve, relationships are healed, and there is greater connection to family and those friends we consider as family. It is exhausting to remain upset, angry, or hurt by the actions of our ancestors. The energy wasted is much better used to create a life we love.

As I sit writing at my desk, I look over from time to time at the framed pictures of some of my female ancestors on the top of my bookcase. I had good relationships with most of my known women ancestors while they were alive. After choosing to practice what I learned in India, I have created "right relationship" with all of them. I have tears in my eyes when I look at their photos now. I know they are thanking and blessing me. I include the ancestors I don't know and am grateful in my heart for their lives, their challenges, and their contributions. I see my own eyes looking back at me when I look at my great-grandmother's eyes, knowing we both embrace the same circle of life.

Ancestors are our best cheerleaders, championing our dreams and guiding us from the other side.

My grandmother Rosie smiles at me from the photo on the bookcase, her eyes gleaming with love and pride. I feel her sending her blessings to everyone whose eyes read these words. I am glad I asked her, and all my ancestors, for help writing this book. We can think of them as our own personal team of fans who think of us like rock stars. Our actions give them a front row seat to the concert of our lives—and our success makes *them* VIPs too. They will be the first to welcome us with enthusiasm when it is our time to pass through to the other side.

Inviting blessings of compassion, forgiveness, and kindness from those who know us in this life liberates us in the next life—and the cycle of evolution and elevation continues for future generations. We send blessings, healing, and love across all generations in this process.

The seven-generation principle taught by Native Americans promotes the stewardship of the world on behalf of the next seven generations. Chris Michaels, of the Center for Spiritual Living in Kansas City, Missouri, goes further to suggest that each of us is "a link in a chain of causation that stretches before and after your life for a thousand generations."[14]

Imagine the tremendous power we have to make our present-day healing bless, honor, and heal generations in both directions—backward and

---

14 Judith Rich, "Healing the Wounds of Your Ancestors," *Huffington Post*, 2011. See http://www.huffingtonpost.com/dr-judith-rich/healing-the-wounds-of-you_b_853632.html.

forward. Our sacred healing tasks will make a difference, gently rendering harmless the hurts of the past and skyrocketing all that is whole and good into the future.

Though many are blessed with loving childhoods, with kind and caring parents, that is not true for everyone. Whether a person had a loving start to life or not, mostly everyone can benefit from taking a look at areas where she or he did not have the love, attention, care, or understanding sought. By actively and consciously giving those gifts to the child within now, wounds that may have occurred in childhood are healed. Bestowing love and attention that was missing in the past, we create a new wholeness and wellbeing.

⚜ ⚜ ⚜

Virtues are the above-the-line qualities, values, and aspects of our behavior that we can choose and feel good about (as discussed in V-Attitude #3). Virtue is clearly aligned with being one's highest and best self, embracing the attributes of humanity that are above the line. A venerable woman shares virtue in the now that imbues all of humanity with a higher resonance.

My friend Ilona, who lives in New Zealand, is part of The Virtues Project—a grassroots initiative to inspire a global revolution of kindness, justice, and integrity in order to transform the world into a more kind and loving one. When she heard I was writing a book about venerable women, she was interested to know what role virtues would play in the book. She sent me a package of printed virtue cards from The Virtues Project. Virtues listed on the beautiful cards included caring, compassion, confidence, cooperation, courage, courtesy, and creativity—and those are just the virtues beginning with the letter *c*! Others included excellence, flexibility, generosity, helpfulness, idealism, kindness, love, loyalty, and unity—reminders of the best attributes of humanity.

I am convinced that humans feel best when they embrace virtue—or more accurately when they *embody* virtue. This is not as hard as it may seem. Each of us is making decisions moment by moment about how we express ourselves in the world. Why not choose virtue?

One of the most beautiful and generous virtues is wisdom. Venerable women are wise. As the definition of *venerable* reminds us, venerable women are worthy of honor, love, and respect by virtue of their *wisdom* and experience.

Wisdom is inherent and wisdom is gained— sometimes through learning from mistakes made, and other times emerging from inner knowing. Divine wisdom is more expansive than anything our minds can imagine—and we can tap into that Divine wisdom when we feel our own wisdom does not go far enough.

Women are willing and worthy bearers of shared wisdom with the world. We share the wisdom of healing, loving, raising children, cooking, teaching, mending hearts, assisting the dying, and the values of tradition. In many cases, females in the family are the ones who remember and act on customs, rituals, and holy and special days.

As a child, I remember not fully understanding the significance of my grandmother Rosie ceremoniously taking out special dishes for holidays. I thought the plates were pretty and wondered why we didn't use them every day. Those dishes were among the very few items packed in a wooden chest and transported to America from Ireland in the 1860s by my grandmother's immigrant family. Each time Rosie carefully placed the treasures on the holiday table, she talked about the McNulty's and their journey to America. I still remember the story fifty years later. Stories and traditions mark a particular time in the circle of life, bring it into the present, and preserve continuity in the future.

My daughters carry on some of the traditions from our family. Though Lauren and Lindsay used to make fun of some customs and traditions when they were younger, it warms my heart to know they embrace them now and add their own touches as well. Sometimes my daughters and I have a good laugh because now *they* are the ones who insist that certain customs and traditions remain constant. Traditions, customs, and rituals are priceless threads that weave generations together. Those who may not have experiences or memories of traditions in their lives can choose to begin new enriching and meaningful traditions of their own. Seven generations back and seven generations forward—healing and celebrating.

In my mind's eye, I see the image of a woman, expansive as the sky, with her arms outstretched encircling all of life on earth with a generous heart and loving ways.

We are all that woman.

"Everyone archetypally is a parent to future generations."

—Marianne Williamson

Transformation
V-Attitude #12

A venerable woman transforms the world by transforming herself, contributing to humanity's evolvement, and interconnecting with all that is.

Transformation starts with self-empowerment. We change our lives for the better by living in deep awareness, fulfilling the needs of our body, mind, spirit, and heart. A new day emerges as we consciously choose to align with our highest and best selves, committed to living "above the line" in our thoughts and actions. We are refreshed by the deep well of our worth, quenching our thirst for honor, love, and respect.

As manifesters and creators, we use our power to conceive a new way of being that is loving and kind. We live in delight with our Divine. Grace emerges in each moment because we are present and alive. We are expressions of the Divine on earth.

Each woman lives in joyful abundance, having what she wants, when she wants it, with plenty left over to share. As we bless each person we encounter, we uplift life to the highest good. We love and are beloved. Our place in the circle of life is a treasure to us, and we honor it in all ways.

When my daughters were little, the three of us would pack a lunch and go to our favorite park reserve in the springtime. The park was magical. One day we discovered a perfectly formed circle of trees. We wondered how the circle of trees came to be so precisely planted since the rest of the park reserve was natural and wild. Standing in the middle of the circle with my young daughters, we made up stories about sacred ceremonies that may have taken place inside the circle or that perhaps it had been a sweet home for faeries.

After many years, I decided to go back to the park reserve, this time with my little dog. We were blessed by one of the first welcome days of warmth after a cold Minnesota winter. Rays of golden sunshine danced on top of crystal-blue ponds, and herons decorated the sky. I'm pretty sure I saw my dog smiling as she hopped along the trails; I know I was smiling as we set off to find the circle of trees. I had a general idea where the trees were and, after a brief search, we came around a bend and there they were!

Much taller now, I ran toward them and greeted my old friends. As I stood in the middle of the circle of trees, I felt an embrace that went deep into my being. Standing within their circle of green, I was inspired and felt the magic and beauty of the world. These trees were wise sisters who stood branch to branch, root to root, year after year, in the fertile soil of love, and remind me of each of *us*—standing in a circle—heart to heart, encircling our world, loving it, and feeling loved in return. We are the venerable women.

We transform the world by transforming ourselves, moment by moment, standing together with others like a forest of wise trees bearing witness and contributing to the evolution of humanity.

"We are your roots, your trunk, your branches. Sit in the shade of our blossom tree and delight in the world you imagine."

—The Collective

THE TWELVE V-ATTITUDES

Relationship with Self

1. *A venerable woman empowers herself* by using inner awareness and fulfilling the needs of her body, mind, spirit, and heart.

2. *A venerable woman embodies her highest and best self* by safeguarding her values, accepting what is, and being authentic.

3. *A venerable woman affirms the depth of her worth* by accessing her finest self, making inspired choices, and doing what is hers to do.

4. *A venerable woman creates and manifests powerfully* by using intention, intuition, and feeling.

Relationship with the Divine

5. *A venerable woman delights in a transcendent relationship with her Divine* by committing to meaningful spiritual practice, receiving fresh inspiration, and living in sacred union.

6. *A venerable woman calls forth grace in each moment* by being present, embracing peace, and engaging fully in life.

7. *A venerable woman lives as an expression of the Divine* by acknowledging the presence of the Divine within her, knowing her soul, and using her gifts.

8. *A venerable woman experiences joyful abundance* by being grateful and generous, and believing in her innate prosperity.

Relationship with Others

9. *A venerable woman uplifts each life she touches* by practicing compassion, unconditional love, and kindheartedness.

10. *A venerable woman loves and is beloved* by inspiring deep connection, trust, and collaboration with others.

11. *A venerable woman embraces the circle of life* by honoring her ancestors and sharing virtue, wisdom, and traditions across generations.

12. *A venerable woman transforms the world* by transforming herself, contributing to humanity's evolvement, and interconnecting with all that is.

To download a printable V-Attitudes poster, go to www.venerablewomen.com and click on the Mini Poster tab.

AFTERWORD

I designed a Venerable Women bracelet for women to wear as an affirmation of their worth. Inside it, a handcrafted inscription reads, "I AM a venerable woman." Each morning I put it on first thing and take a moment to remind myself to *be* that woman, remembering I am worthy of honor, love, and respect—and to do what is mine to do to keep that sentiment true. Throughout the day, it reminds me to send a blessing to every woman who is committed to live *her* highest and best life, or who is awakening to its call in her soul. In this simple act, I feel connected at a heart level to each one who is choosing to transform the world.

The way a venerable woman, or any person who chooses to, transforms the world is by changing her or his own life for the better. An energetic shift occurs because the person who transforms in positive ways resonates at a higher level of happiness, contentment, and fulfillment in tangible ways. This resonance expands out and out, person by person, causing a ripple-in-the-pond effect of delicious interactions that include support, understanding, compassion, and connection. Quite simply, there is more love, and there is more peace inside the one who transforms and within each life she touches.

Another way that an individual's personal transformation changes the world for the better is even more profound than raising the vibrational energy—and that other way is to break the chain of bad behavior. Many of us believe in our souls that humanity can be freed, liberated, and emancipated from all bonds of unloving and unkind acts. I believe that is why many of us are here and are choosing this path at this time on earth. We are here to manifest a kind and loving world together across generations.

I have come to accept that each person chooses and ultimately does best when taking responsibility for all that she or he has experienced in this life. Whatever has happened to us has been so that we could awaken to all we are called to be—and we rise above *because* of those circumstances. We are not, and never have been victims, though it may have felt that way before we awakened. If one believes in God or the Divine or a Higher Power, do we think that higher power would cause us suffering? No, absolutely not. *We* voluntarily chose our circumstances ourselves so we could evolve.

In my own family, a chain of bad behavior in the form of abandonment, high drama, untrustworthiness, and a host of other undesirable traits left in their wake much pain and suffering. I have seen various versions of deep pain and suffering in others' lives too.

Each of us is doing the best we know to do, and if one has hurt another, it is out of that person's own internal pain. Happy and fulfilled people, who feel they are loved and commit to be as whole as they can be, do not hurt others intentionally. Internal pain deserves understanding and compassion. We are capable of rising to that level, and are called to do so. If our lives are one big play, with everyone playing her or his role—I know that, at the end of the play, *everyone* gets a standing ovation. All lives are interconnected and work together for humanity's evolution.

When one clearly sees what is longing to be healed and understood, at whatever point in life it occurs, and then commits to see the message of evolution inside—that is when true and generous transformation happens.

The mother who loses her son in an accident caused by a drunk driver, and chooses to forgive the driver, transforms herself and breaks a chain of hatred. The adult who heals from childhood sexual abuse clears the path for healthy relationships for future generations of his family. The woman who felt unloved and unwanted by her father in her childhood and can now see how her father was a product of all that had happened in his own life, learns to love all that she *can* love and appreciate about him. By feeling compassion for his disappointments and the lack of love *he* needed and did not get, she breaks a sordid chain of family separation and generational strife.

To extract the blessing from the challenge is a sacred act—and the most liberating thing we can do for ourselves and for our world. We are ready. It is our time.

I will not die an unlived life.
I will not live in fear of falling or catching fire.
I choose to inhabit my days, to
allow my living to open me,
to make me less afraid, more accessible,
to loosen my heart until it becomes
a wing, a torch, a promise.

—Dawna Markova, PhD

P.S. to Men

I received a Facebook message from a man who read my blog:

"I noticed how real and aware of life and personal evolvement you are. However, I feel left out somehow. If you were ever inclined to widen your scope of projection to sharing with say venerable *people*, I would appreciate that. It may end up sparing me the time and effort of dressing in drag at some point to gain access or acceptance to your seminars and events."

I responded, "Because of your message, I immediately bought the domain names venerablepeople.com and venerablemen.com. I want to be more inclusive. I am looking at a model to inspire all people, both men and women—and children, too. At a conference I attended (Future First Women's Congress), the women agreed to take responsibility for action to save our planet—from a women's perspective. They asked the men who attended to participate, share, support, and witness. It was a beautiful event. I will continue to look at how to honor and inspire both women and men. Many people are now ready to be the light-bearers of a way of being that is col-laborative, kind, nurturing, inclusive, and non-com-petitive. Thank you again for your wisdom and for reaching out. And you do not have to dress like a woman to attend Venerable Women events and ben-efit from these concepts—unless that's your thing!"

❧ ❧ ❧

To each of the men who are consciously evolving and supporting the women and girls in their own lives, I thank you. You are a blessing to the world. You are our venerable men.

Suggested Reading

Abraham, Esther Hicks, and Jerry Hicks. *Ask and It Is Given: Learning to Manifest Your Desires.* Carlsbad, CA: Hay House, 2004.

Cameron, Julia. *The Artist's Way: A Spiritual Path to Higher Creativity.* New York: J.P. Tarcher/Putnam, 2002.

Cavendish, Richard. "Woman." *Man Myth & Magic: An Illustrated Encyclopedia of the Supernatural.* Italy: BPC Publishing Ltd., 1970.

Chödrön, Pema, and Joan Duncan Oliver. *Living Beautifully with Uncertainty and Change.* Boston: Shambhala, 2012.

Christ, Carol. *The Laughter of Aphrodite.* San Francisco: Harper and Row, 1988.

Condren, Mary. *The Serpent and the Goddess: Women Religion and Power in Celtic Ireland.* San Francisco: Harper & Row Publishers, 1989.

Ehrenreich, Barbara, and Deirdre English. *Witches, Midwives, and Nurses: A History of Women Healers.* New York: The Feminist Press, 1973.

Eisler, Riane. *The Chalice & the Blade: Our History Our Future.* San Francisco: Harper & Row, 1988.

Flanagan, Sabina. *Hildegard of Bingen: A Visionary Life.* New York: Barnes and Noble Books, 1999.

Gilbert, Elizabeth. *Big Magic: Creative Living beyond Fear.* New York: Bloomsbury Publishing, 2015.

Gimbutas, Marija. *Language of the Goddess.* San Francisco: Harper & Row, 1989.

Karlson, Carol. *The Devil in the Shape of a Woman.* New York: Vintage Books, 1989.

Kidd, Sue Monk. *The Dance of the Dissident Daughter: A Woman's Journey from Christian Tradition to the Sacred Feminine.* San Francisco: HarperSanFrancisco, 1996.

Kondō, Marie, and Cathy Hirano. *The Life-Changing Magic of Tidying Up: The Japanese Art of Decluttering and Organizing.* New York: Ten Speed Press, 2014.

LeGendre, Lyn. "The Witch Hunt: Another form of female persecution?" *North Shore Magazine* 26 Dec. 1991: 8, 15.

McLaren, Karla. *The Language of Emotions: What Your Feelings Are Trying to Tell You.* Boulder: Sounds True, 2010.

Redgrove, Peter, and Penelope Shuttle. *The Wise Wound: Myths Realities and Meanings of Menstruation.* New York: Bantam Books, 1986.

Sandberg, Sheryl. *Lean In: Women, Work, and the Will to Lead.* New York: Knopf, 2013.

Starbird, Margaret. *The Woman with the Alabaster Jar: Mary Magdalen and the Holy Grail.* Santa Fe: Bear & Company, 1993.

Stone, Merlin. *When God Was a Woman.* New York: Harcourt Brace Jovanovich, Publishers, 1976.

Tolle, Eckhart. *Practicing the Power of Now: Essential Teachings, Meditations, and Exercises from the Power of Now.* Novato, CA: New World Library, 1999.

Ulrich, Laurel Thatcher. *A Midwife's Tale.* New York: Vintage Books, 1990.

Walsch, Neale Donald. *Conversations with God: An Uncommon Dialogue.* Norfolk, VA: Hampton Roads Pub., 1997.

Wheatley, Margaret J. *Turning to One Another: Simple Conversations to Restore Hope to the Future.* San Francisco, CA: Berrett-Koehler, 2002.

Wilde, Dana *Train Your Brain: How to Build a Million Dollar Business in Record Time,* Balboa Press, 2013

Williams, Selma. *Riding the Nightmare: Women & Witchcraft from the Old World to Colonial Salem.* New York: HarperPerennial, 1992.

Williamson, Marianne. *A Woman's Worth*. New York: Random House, 1993.

Zander, Rosamund Stone, and Benjamin Zander. *The Art of Possibility*. Boston: Harvard Business School, 2000.

ACKNOWLEDGMENTS

Thank you, Betty Beebe, the sister I choose, who sends waves of love to me in immeasurable ways. My gratitude goes to Janet Fischer, my darling real, true, and constant friend. Thank you, Ruth Godfrey, founder of Learning Journeys International Center of Coaching, who taught me the exquisite principles of life coaching that changed my life—and positively impacted the lives of those I coach.

Thank you, my dear friend, my spiritual sojourner and curator of inspiration, Jeanette Monterio. We traveled to India together and shared profound transformations at Oneness University— where, over a month, I was stripped to the core, inspired, and profoundly affirmed. I can think of no one I'd rather have had that experience with.

My gratitude and love to Reverend Sandra McKinney for personifying integrity—and for being a master at promoting women's new ventures in the world.

My heartfelt gratitude goes to Reverend Audrey Peterson who speaks truth and inspires beauty, and

Reverend Barbara Winter Martin who lives in alignment with her highest self.

Gratitude and love to Dianne Moore, AKA Petunia, who brings me to higher expression and joy in more ways than I knew existed—and is always a walk, a phone call, or a thought away.

Thank you, Rebecca Airmet, for walking the Venerable Women path with me and sharing your brilliance and many gifts.

Julie Delene, thank you for embodying movement and co-creation in my life. Thank you Dana Wilde, for taking me under your generous and beautiful wings; and for Joan Kremer, my longtime friend who left this world, yet never leaves my side as I write. Tatjana Zemkuznikov, Sheila Wines, Reverend Dr. Patricia Keel, Maggie Chula, Mary Welch, Laurie Harper, Susan Cevette, Linda Ruhland, Laura Davida Preves, Judith Krauthamer, Aly Meech, Kat Menaged, Jen Grant, Coco Daniels, Dawn Vogel, and all the Liberal Chicks, I thank you for the unique ways you each support my work and me.

A deep and profound thank you goes to my darling friend and collaborator, Carole Hyder, who transforms inner and outer spaces into beautiful ones.

Thank you, Women's Weekend friends and partners: Janet Fischer, Kathy Brown, Paula Weber, Roberta Haight, Sue Brenny, Bette Schmit, Ruth Bettendorf, Mary Sue Binsfeld, Jody Buell, Patti Jo Cwodzinski, Chris Goldade, Diane Reynolds, Lani

Haire, Stephanie Roy, Anne Foslid, Ann Meyer, and Denise Fletcher, who opened your hearts and arms to me when I first moved to Minnesota from the East Coast and continue the tradition as we move through our lives.

Thank you, Gina Wilkinson, my witty and longtime friend who continues to remind me that when I was nineteen years old I told her I wanted to do something with my life that would help women.

A warm and loving acknowledgment to Patric von Drashek who showed me abundantly that there are good and decent men in the world who love, honor, and respect women. And thank you, Dr. Paul Burgio, for your generosity of time, guidance, and information.

I extend a joyful and endearing acknowledgment to Aaron Klemm, my daughter Lauren's husband, who is a son I am grateful to have in my life, and to Nils Johnson, my daughter Lindsay's enlightened choice of partner.

Gratitude and love to Stephen Calvit who does great work in the world for the dying, and who supports and loves me fully.

My heartfelt love and gratitude goes to Mischa Warren and Mark Goggin and their sons Hugo and Blake, for adding more love and joy to the story of my life.

Thank you, Pat Fischer, watching over us from the other side. Your integrity, kindness, and love, gifted everyone who had the joy of knowing you.

A dear and grateful heart hug goes to my father, Arthur Morningstar, who shared a song with me that I still hum in my heart to this day.

Thank you, Bill Gladstone, literary agent and publisher, for your enlightened view of our world, and for your integrity.

I am most grateful to my extraordinary editor, Marly Cornell, who skillfully dove with me into deep waters of words and helped me pull up the big treasures.

My gratitude goes to Joel Hodroff, founder of DualCurrency Systems, who shared his exceptional coaching skills with me.

Blessings and love to Doris Morningstar and Cierra and Sophia Kopecky.

I have deep love and abiding gratitude for my venerable daughters, Lauren and Lindsay. You are the sun, rain, and fertile soil for the seeds of my highest and best self. I loved every phase of raising the two of you—from the time I looked into your newborn eyes, fresh from the Divine, to this present day as you stand in the world as lovely young women. I trusted the wisdom I knew was inherent in you, bubbling up to the surface and ever present. My mother heart overflows with appreciation.

I thank my mother, Vicky Morningstar, who inspired both pain and possibility. Had she not abandoned me as a child, and had I had a "normal" sweet childhood, this awakening to serve, inspire, and connect women might not have occurred. Her absence was the grain of sand in the oyster. Love, forgiveness, fear, change, compassion, and unworthiness layered and layered upon the grain. I find myself ever grateful for the resulting pearl that became Venerable Women. My mother's soul agreement inspired this opportunity for all women to remember and proclaim themselves pearls of inestimable value—and to love and respect themselves from a deep, rich seabed of self-worth.

Thank you, dear Collective, for opening the circle to each of us and sharing your wisdom.

ABOUT THE AUTHOR

Dawn Morningstar is a master coach, educator, former radio talk show host, and the grateful mother of two venerable daughters. Dawn worked as an account executive for a national staffing agency in Washington, DC, and as a trainer for an international skincare company. She has a Master Coach Certification from Learning Journeys, The International Center of Coaching. As a heart-centered entrepreneur, she launched two businesses: one that provided fundraising for public schools, daycare centers, and nonprofits, and the other coaching clients ready to live their highest and best lives. In 2007 Dawn coauthored *Delicious Conversations: Arriving at Unexpected Moments of Joy* (Gathering House) with Ruth M. Godfrey. Dawn founded Venerable Women in 2013 as an organization, a philosophy, and a movement with and for women who choose to manifest a kind and loving world, starting within themselves.

Dawn lives in St. Paul, Minnesota, with her little dog, Pica.